Honest Faith for Our Time

Honest Faith for Our Time

Truth-telling about the Bible, the Creed, and the Church

J. Harold Ellens

☙PICKWICK *Publications* · Eugene, Oregon

HONEST FAITH FOR OUR TIME
Truth-telling about the Bible, the Creed, and the Church

Copyright © 2010 J. Harold Ellens. All rights reserved. Except for brief quotations in critical publications or reviews, no part of this book may be reproduced in any manner without prior written permission from the publisher. Write: Permissions, Wipf and Stock Publishers, 199 W. 8th Ave., Suite 3, Eugene, OR 97401.

Pickwick Publications
An Imprint of Wipf and Stock Publishers
199 W. 8th Ave., Suite 3
Eugene, OR 97401

www.wipfandstock.com

ISBN 13: 978-1-60899-708-4

Cataloguing-in-Publication data:

Ellens, J. Harold, 1932–.

    Honest faith for our time : truth-telling about the Bible, the creed, and the church / J. Harold Ellens ; with contributions by Jack Miles, James M. Robinson, and F. Morgan Roberts.

    xiv + 180 pp. ; 23 cm. Includes bibliographical references and index.

    ISBN 13: 978-1-60899-708-4

    1. Christianity. 2. Apostles' Creed. I. Miles, Jack, 1942–. II. Robinson, James M. (James McConkey), 1924–. III. Roberts, F. Morgan. IV. Title.

BR121.2 .E40 2010

Manufactured in the U.S.A.

*This book is for
Brett Alexander Ellens Hutchison,
my dearly beloved son,
the bright and cheering grace gifted me
by a provident and grace-filled God,
for the consolations and care
of my old age.*

Contents

The Apostles' Creed / ix
Preface / xi

PART ONE: The Creed and the Church

1. I Believe in God / 3
2. Jesus Christ, Our Lord / 9
3. Conceived of the Spirit, Born of a Virgin / 16
4. Suffered, Died, Buried / 22
5. He Descended into Hell / 26
6. He Rose from the Dead / 31
7. Ascended and Enthroned Judge / 37
8. Holy Spirit: Universal Church, Saintly Communion, Fellowship of Forgiveness / 44
9. Resurrection of the Body / 51
10. Life Everlasting / 56

PART TWO: How the Divine Spirit Really Works in Our Daily Lives

11. Honest to God / 63
12. Why I Believe in God / 70
13. The Backside of God / 76

PART THREE: How the Divine Spirit Really Works in the Church

14. Healthy Faith Needs Good Theology / 89

15	Wellbeing: God's Grace and Human Health / 95
16	Responsible Religion, Honest Theology, Good Grace / 105
17	The Chemistry of Forgiveness / 115

PART FOUR: Summary and Conclusion

18	A Godly Way of Life / 125

PART FIVE: Three Responses

19	Bible before Creed or Creed before Bible—Jack Miles / 137
20	From the Apostles' Creed to Jesus' Own Trust in God —James M. Robinson / 143
21	A Pastor's Response—F. Morgan Roberts / 154

About the Author and Respondents / 171

Suggestions for Further Reading / 174

Bibliography / 177

Index / 179

The Apostles' Creed

I believe in God the father, almighty maker of heaven and earth;
and in Jesus Christ his only begotten son, our Lord;
Who was conceived of the Holy Spirit,
born of the Virgin Mary,
suffered under Pontius Pilate,
was crucified, died, and was buried.
He descended into hell.
The third day he arose again from the dead,
ascended into heaven,
and is seated on the right hand of God the father.
From thence he shall come to judge the living and the dead.
I believe in the Holy Spirit,
the Holy Catholic Church,
the communion of Saints,
the forgiveness of sins,
the resurrection of the body,
and the life everlasting.

Preface

Fifty-five years ago I was a graduate student of Professors Bruce M. Metzger and Otto Piper at Princeton Theological Seminary. I proposed to Metzger that I write my thesis on the authority of Scripture, expecting him to admire the idea. Instead, without any dialogue, he said I could do that if I insisted, but I would need to move to the theology department, since New Testament Studies was not really interested in the topic. I was stunned. I chose, almost on the spot, not to write a thesis but rather to take the extra courses one could substitute, since I concluded from Metzger's peremptory statement that there was a lot I still had to learn about biblical studies.

However, my perplexity about why Metzger would have responded in that fashion continued to provoke me so I asked Professor Piper, at one of the Thursday afternoon student teas he and Mrs. Piper hosted at their home, how he grounded the authority of the Christian faith for his own personal, as well as his theological satisfaction. His response was as surprising to me in my naiveté at the time, as was Metzger's, though it was much more helpful. Piper said in a gracious and humorously pastoral way, "Well, when in your personal dialogue with life you find that the ancient testimony of Scripture seems to be expressed in the confessions of the historic church, and so the witness of the ancient community in the Bible and the witness in the Church's tradition of belief, rings true to your own personal experience of faith, then I suppose you might be right to consider yourself on fairly solid ground."

That wise counsel has guided me ever since. It certified my confidence in the authenticity and freedom of my personal spiritual quest. It delivered me from a bondage to the sacred Scripture while strengthening my profound appreciation for the word of grace within it. It freed me to critique the historic tradition of the creeds and confessions of the church. It empowered me to be a creative biblical scholar, theologian, preacher, and pastor.

I have now worked vigorously with the biblical text, the church's faith-claims, and my own psychospirituality for much more than a half century. It has been a demanding, sometimes painful, always illumining, and perpetually gratifying journey. After so long a time of diligent and responsible reflections one has earned the right to give a warrantable testimony to the truth, wisdom, and knowledge one has experienced. This volume is my testimony regarding one central facet of that journey: my perceptions regarding the truths and troubles of the Christian faith in the light of the New Testament Scriptures and the church's most familiar creed.

There is an important reason that one should give a clear testimony about one's confession after a life of faith and work with the Bible and the creeds of the Church. That reason arises from the fact that most of us Christians read the Scriptures and recite the Apostles' Creed every Sunday in our worship liturgy. The church has done so throughout most of its two millennia of history. It is easy to do that as a routine exercise with little thought to the amazing truth-claims the Church's creeds make in their attempt to interpret the New Testament. It is easy to do this without any discernment as to what those claims mean to us personally. Are they really *our* truth-claims? What do we really mean by them? Do we really believe what the words and propositions of the Creed literally declare? Do they really have any connection to the actual truth about God? Does the New Testament really shine clearly through the rather brief and cryptic summary of the faith that we call The Apostles' Creed? Do its truth-claims have anything to do with shaping the character and quality of our lives?

The Apostles' Creed was written in an effort to impose Greek definitions upon the Church's understanding of God and upon the Hebrew metaphors of the Bible. The Bible tells us about God in pictures that are formulated in the patterns of human experiences, relationships, images, ideas, and stories. So we talk about God in human language and use human images to describe God. We refer to God as father, friend, caregiver, creator, lover, savior, and comforter.

The bishops who wrote the creeds wanted to do better than the Bible. They wanted to define God. It did not work as well as they thought it would. As a result, many Christians in the twenty-first century find themselves reciting the Apostles' Creed each Sunday morning in a routine way that does not pay any attention to the meaning of the far too familiar words; or they find themselves troubled with specific claims of the Creed that do not seem to square with the Bible or make good sense in our current daily life. Surely the apostles would not recognize that creed as their statement of Christian faith.

I would like to begin this study of honest faith for the twenty-first century by a careful examination of that creed that we call the Apostles' Creed and then move on to some of the main themes of the New Testament story about Jesus, and about the Holy Spirit, which Jesus so plainly stated in John 14 would permanently replace him in this world. I have prepared these reflections on the Apostles' Creed in the form of ruminations for modern-day, thinking Christians, in order to provoke a sense of freedom on the part of devoted Christians who want a clear sense of the biblically based faith and who struggle with the routine recitation of the creed, as well as those faithful Christians who find themselves mumbling through some of the creed's phrases, as I do, because they are not convinced of their actual truth.

On the one hand, I would like to assist the believing community to see the Apostles' Creed as an important document in the long history of the church's struggle to understand the faith. On the other hand, I would like to illumine our faith tradition by clarifying that this Creed is a document that should be taken as no more than an historical artifact, representing only one ancient and temporary phase of the church's quest to understand its professed faith. The Apostles' Creed should be seen as a formulation of faith from a long-ago age and culture, which offers us, nonetheless, surprisingly good insights, but carries with it deficits that should not be allowed to obstruct the free expressions of our spirits today, as we try to lift our hearts and voices to God in faith.

There is much in the creeds to affirm and much against which to react. In both of those aspects of authentic wrestling with the quest of faith lies the potential for great personal spiritual growth. If we are honest in that quest we will not lose our grip on the mystery of the biblical faith, nor accept blind faith as a true connection with God and God's truth. Piper was right. We must avail ourselves of the open-ended quest for God's truth; and when in our personal dialogue with life we find that the ancient testimony of the biblical scriptures seems to be expressed in the confessions and creeds of the historic church, and all that rings true to our own personal experience of the life of faith, then we might be right to consider ourselves on fairly solid ground.

—J. Harold Ellens
Advent 2009

PART ONE

The Creed and the Church

1

I Believe in God

INTRODUCTION

There are many good reasons to study the Bible, and particularly to read its opening narrative. In its original Hebrew language that story in the first chapter of Genesis is one of the most exquisite poems preserved from ancient times in archaic Hebrew script. It is a rewriting of an ancient Mesopotamian myth, the original text of which can be discerned behind the biblical text as we have it today. The Hebrew poem is infinitely more beautiful than typical ancient Mesopotamian documents. Probably only the core parts of the Book of Job are more archaic and more exquisite ancient Hebrew poetry than Genesis 1. One reason to read the Bible might simply be to study Genesis 1, just to celebrate the beauty of that text.

Another reason one might find great relish in exploring Genesis 1 as a subject for scholarly inquiry or homiletic reflection is because it presents such a colorfully stated narrative of the ages of evolution that God employed as his mode and method for creating the material world. I often wonder how the ancient poet(s) who wrote Genesis 1 knew so much about the scientific nature of this large world of nearly infinite universes. Genesis 1 tells a story of what we might call Theistic Evolution, that is, God's designed and expedited process of the development, by evolution, of the all universes that constitute our world, and of everything that is therein, including humankind. There is a lot of sound and fury these days regarding the opinions of the Creationists, the Intelligent Design promoters, and the secular evolutionists. This is a completely absurd debate. Most of that sound and fury signifies nothing of importance.

Anyone who reads Genesis 1 attentively cannot avoid seeing that it describes in poetic detail a kind of developmental process of progressive stages and ages, comparable to what scientists have carefully outlined as the pattern of the evolution of our material world. Darwin surely liked Genesis 1. The Bible story refers to six days of creation. The Hebrew word for day that is used there is *Yom*. It is the word used elsewhere in the Bible to refer to such things as the day of Hezekiah, or the day Jeremiah. It means an era of time of undefined length. The creationists who refuse to see this and insist instead upon a radical contrast between creation and evolution are ignorant. They just do not deal with the facts. Their information base is incomplete.

Evolutionists who miss the facts of intelligent design in creation and the necessity of a creative mind behind all that, are not being very smart either. They not only lack the data to rule out God's creative role in evolution; but refuse to receive an adequate theory to rule it in, namely, that of theistic evolution. It is worse than ignorance to refuse to consider truth or wisdom that is available and fairly obvious. It is a kind of arrogance. Ignorance can be fixed with education. Arrogant ignorance resists all repairs.

Secondly, one might consider studying Genesis 1 because in the 26th verse we have what theologians used to call the Cultural Mandate. "Be fruitful and multiply and replenish the earth, and have dominion over it." There is God's command for us to take care of our world and make it pay off with all the potentials and possibilities for creative development with which God has endowed it. Genesis 1:26 outlines both our authority and responsibility regarding the material world. God has given it into our hands. He does not intend to intervene to protect it and make it achieve its optimal ends. He has assigned us that task!

GOD, THE FATHER, ALMIGHTY CREATOR

So there are many reasons to read or carefully study Genesis 1, as well as the rest of the Bible, for scholarly or devotional purposes. However, I wish to draw attention to this marvelous biblical poetry at this point for none of those reasons. My reason is that I wish in this chapter to share some reflections upon the Apostles' Creed and how it got the way it is. The first line in the creed declares, "I believe in God the father, almighty, maker of heaven and earth." This is taken directly from Genesis 1:1,

"In the beginning God created the heavens and the earth." So these two passages, from scripture and the creed are closely linked.

Human beings, it seems, are theologians, whether we know it, like it, intend it, understand it, or not. We all find percolating up in our minds and hearts in various ways, throughout our daily existence, the essential questions theologians live a lifetime asking. That is, we are all persons who consciously or unconsciously long to know about God. We desire intently to *know* God, and want to get everything about God the right way around. We hunger for good answers to the right theological questions. Believers and unbelievers alike are all theologians. This chapter is about interested believers, who do not have the privilege of being highly skilled Bible scholars, but naturally inquire into the issues and questions of true faith. It is about non-professional theologians pursuing theological inquiry, that is, searching for honest knowledge about God.

All of us are by nature theologians. That is, we all are wired in such a way, so to speak, that we find ourselves spontaneously asking questions about God's nature and behavior. We all want to know what we can honestly count on from God, and therefore what our lives mean. That makes us all natural theologians. Being a theologian is hard work. First of all, one needs to take the Bible seriously and work out a rather thorough understanding of it. The Apostles' Creed was created for many reasons, one of which was to assist the inquiring Christian to work out that essential understanding of the Bible. It is hard work to get a substantial understanding of the facts and ideas of the Bible, and to figure out what the theological meanings are in all of that.

One of the remarkable things about the first line of the Apostles' Creed is the fact that it is the only article of the 12 articles of faith in the creed that was not hotly contested by the delegates to the ancient Ecumenical Councils of the 4th and 5th centuries, when the creed was formulated. That process of formulating the creeds of the Church lasted from the Council of Nicea in 325 CE to that of Chalcedon in 451 CE. Those bishops who attended these councils all agreed that the foundation and cornerstone on which everything else in biblical faith depended was the affirmation, "I believe in God the father, almighty, creator of heaven and earth."

To discern the remarkable differences of theological judgment shaping the debates that prevailed at those councils, one needs only compare the tortured lines of the Apostles' Creed, of the Athanasian

Creed, and of the Nicene Creed. If we compare their language we can discern the implied effort the bishops expended to get things just right. The first article is pretty much the same in all three, but none of the other eleven articles is the same in all three creeds. The differences indicate how widely debated the exact wording of the foundational statements of our faith really were among all those bishops who gathered at the great church councils in the fourth and fifth centuries after Christ.

Of course, you might say that it is no surprise that they agreed on this first line. What other options did they really have but to affirm that the created world came from the creative hand of God? Well, the case is that this affirmation in the fourth and fifth centuries was a radical claim for the Christian community to make. Christianity arose in the rich and fertile world of Greek and Roman philosophy and theology. The Greeks and Romans held that the material world had either generated itself or existed from all eternity, and that it would continue forever. Some of them thought of this world as a kind of divine organism, alive with the nature and spirit of God. They did not see God as an agent apart from the material world, who had, by an act of will, created the world as a form of existence separate from God's self. They thought of the world as God's body or material manifestation, and the life force in the world as the divine soul or spirit.

It is an intriguing and worthy question to ask, of course, in what sense those Greeks and Romans were close to the truth and in what sense they were far from it. Baruch Spinoza and Friedrich Schleiermacher had some genuine appreciation for that Greco-Roman perspective. They found something to appreciate in the ancient notion of the world infused with the divine spirit. But the theologians who formulated the creeds wanted to say that God is separate from God's creation. God is an agent of wisdom and action who exists "out there," outside this world, so to speak; and God decided by a willful and mindful act to create the world that we know, experience, and explore.

That is what the first line of the creed intends to affirm. God, who exists "out there," sired this world, as a father does, and acts as an independent agent in creation, providence, and the guidance of all things to their appointed ends. John Calvin, the great Swiss Reformer of the sixteenth century defined the essence of our faith as "a sure knowledge of God and of God's promises and a certain (unquestioned) confidence that God directs all things to their appointed ends."

I have felt for a long time that there are five reasons to believe in God. I believe in God because of the 1) mindfulness of creation, 2) the aesthetic urge in all things in the universe, which always seem to be moving toward beauty, 3) the benevolence of providence in which even our pain fosters our growth, 4) the unique relevance of unconditional grace to our particular need as limited human beings, and 5) the fact that God insinuates himself in surprising ways into individual histories. None of these, of course, speaks especially of Jesus, the Christ. Jesus, the Christ, is not a reason to believe in God. Believing in God is a reason to believe in Jesus, as the Christ.

Jesus, as the Christ, is one of the elements of the content of Christian faith. There are those five reasons *why* one should believe in God; and there are three things concerning *what* to believe about God: 1) God is manifest as the Father and creator in the material universes; 2) God is manifested as the Son, our brother, in Jesus, the Christ, a specific man who lived at a specific moment in history; and 3) God is present in our world today as Divine Spirit, present in our spirits, in the spirit of the church, *and in the world*. That is what the Apostles' Creed correctly claims.

The theology that is proclaimed by the first verse of Genesis 1 and by the first article of the creed is, interestingly, a creationist theology and not an atonement theology. The church has spent the last 20 centuries preoccupied with atonement theology. It has been trying to answer the question as to why and how Jesus' spilled blood, on a Roman cross, on a dusty Palestinian hill, outside of a virtually unknown village, in a virtually irrelevant country, 2000 years ago, redeems us. However, the first verse of the Bible and the first article of the creed do not deal with such issues as the resolution of the problem of sin or alienation from God. Neither did the first great Christian theologian after St. Paul. Irenaeus of Lyon crafted his entire theological model around a creation-based theology. He believed God created the world, and the entire scope of history in which God's world was to unfold, and that the entire process of things was like a large envelope of God's unfolding work. It began, it burgeons, and it draws to a redemptive close.

God began with the First Adam who was the starter, as in sourdough bread, but he was not the completed loaf, and God's work stretched all the way to the Second Adam, namely Jesus, the Christ, who completed and consummated the total envelope of God's dynamic creating. Irenaeus referred to this envelope as God's economy, that is, the life-history of God's household. Irenaeus saw this as a sort of closed system of divine creating in this world and its history. You and I, who have come along 2000 years after the days of the Christ, are simply living in the age of the Holy Spirit, enjoying God's work of grace and providence, celebrating the security and certain assurance of God's *already completed* saving activity. We live in the spirit-flood flowing from the wellspring of God's economy. We live out of the intimations of the Spirit, according to Irenaeus, which can fill our lives with God's presence. If we have the eyes to see and the ears to hear; we can live life watching how God will show up around the next corner in our personal and communal life.

This notion of Irenaeus would not have been a strange or foreign sound to St. Paul, who saw the work of God's redeeming presence in history as moving forcefully from the first big bang of creation to the second big bang of Pentecost; from the beginning of life in Genesis 1 to the new life in the Spirit of the Christ in the New Testament. Paul was sure that this was what was always giving divine meaning to this world and its unfolding history. Surely, that is exactly what John 1:1–3 intends for us to see, as well, as it virtually repeats the framework of thought of Genesis 1. There is really no atonement theology in the Fourth Gospel. It starts right out with the declaration that Jesus, the Christ, is the container of the creative force of God. John calls that force the *Logos* of God. The Gospel of John declares from the outset that "In the beginning was the *Logos*, and the *Logos* was with God; and God was the *Logos*. All things were made by the *Logos* and without him was nothing made that was made. In the *Logos* was life and that life was the light for humankind." *Logos* means God's articulate expression of God's nature and behavior.

The Hebrew Bible refers to the *Logos* as the personified force of Wisdom. It is *Chokmah* in Hebrew and *Sophia* in Greek. According to John, this force of creative Wisdom that was already acting in Genesis was incarnated in Jesus, the Christ. So John can say (1:3) "All things were made by him, and without him was not anything made that was made." So to live a life in Bible study, one must begin at the beginning, in Genesis 1, and in the first article of the Apostles' Creed, "I believe in God the father, almighty, maker of heaven and earth!" Then, with Iranaeus, one must look for the consummation of God's creative history in the Second Adam. "In the beginning God . . . in the end God in Christ . . . the hope of the world!" (John 1:1–3, 14).

2

Jesus Christ, Our Lord

THE SECOND ARTICLE OF the Apostles' Creed is "I believe in Jesus Christ, God's unique son, our Lord." That confession of faith surely finds its central grounding in John 3:16–17, where we read that God so loved the world, which he created, that he sent his unique son to save it, not to condemn it. In the mid-nineteenth century Pope Pius IX, a very politically-oriented pope with a great sense of mission to change the institutions and social conditions of our world, declared as official dogma the doctrine of the Immaculate Conception and the Bodily Assumption of Mary, Jesus' mother.

He was not very concerned about whether these doctrines were historically true. He was interested in the fact that they were politically advantageous for gluing the power of the papacy to the membership of the Roman Catholic Church worldwide. He undoubtedly agreed with Pope Leo X of the sixteenth century. Regarding the question of whether Jesus ever really existed or what he was really like, Leo declared that the *myth of Jesus* had stood the church in very good stead since the first century after Christ, implying that, therefore, there was no good reason to question or disturb it, whether it was historically authentic or not.

From the very beginning of Jesus' ministry, however, and therefore from the very beginning of the Christian Movement, there was an intense struggle to understand Jesus, that person from that place and that time. Those who witnessed his ministry and heard him preach in their synagogue asked, "Is not this the son of Joseph, the Carpenter?" The formulators of the Apostles' Creed declared, "We believe in Jesus Christ, God's unique son, our Lord."

That quest to fix Jesus as a man in that time and that place 2,000 years ago, has persisted as a preoccupation of Christians ever since. For the last hundred and fifty years scholars have engaged in what has been called "the Quest of the Historical Jesus." That was begun by an eighteenth-century German theologian named Reimarus, followed by such important nineteenth-century German professors as Johannes Weiss, Albrecht Ritschl, and David Friedrich Strauss. A critical turning point in this attempt to track down Jesus and identify him, once and for all, was reached by the work of Albert Schweitzer. He took up the Quest for the Historical Jesus in earnest, concluding in the end that he had figured out who Jesus really was.[1] He determined that Jesus was a Galilean mystic. Schweitzer worried about whether Jesus was, perhaps, somewhat delusional. He concluded that Jesus was certainly naive in his ideas about the coming of God's kingdom on earth, and wrong about his own second coming at the end of time.

Between World War I and World War II, Rudolf Bultmann critiqued Schweitzer's claim. In the 1950s, Professor James M. Robinson evaluated the quest from Reimarus to Bultmann; he summarized and evaluated the discussion among the post-Bultmannian group of German scholars and identified what he called the *New Quest for the Historical Jesus*. They proposed to take more seriously the essence of what Jesus really said and did, as evidence of who he was and what he was up to.

Robinson joined a group of about sixty scholars who formed The Jesus Seminar. You have read about it in *Time Magazine* and the newspapers. They set as their task the attempt to read every word of the four gospels and determine which were authentic words from Jesus and descriptions of his actual behavior, and which were later added as interpretation by Jesus' followers, after his death and resurrection.

The Jesus Seminar worked for over six years and produced a document that indicated what the scholars were sure were the specific words right from the mouth of Jesus himself. That selection of Jesus sayings is known to scholars as *The Five Gospels: The Search for the Authentic Words of Jesus*.[2] The Gospels of Matthew and Luke not only copied the earlier Gospel of Mark, but they also seem to have used a source that Mark did not know about. That was what we now call the Sayings Gospel Q. There were other sayings gospels, such as the much later *Gospel of Thomas*, but

---

1. Albert Schweitzer, *The Quest of the Historical Jesus*, first complete edition, trans. W. Montgomery et al., ed. John Bowden, Fortress Classics in Biblical Studies (Minneapolis: Fortress, 2001).

2. Robert W. Funk et al., *The Five Gospels: The Search for the Authentic Words of Jesus* (New York: Macmillan, 1993).

the Sayings Gospel Q seems to give us the essence of who Jesus really was and what he really said. Robinson was convinced, on the basis of the testimony of both the Gospel of Mark and the Sayings Gospel Q, that Jesus was not delusional but was an ascetic who laid his life on the line to proclaim the possibility and imperative of God's kingdom of love and grace on this earth. He was sure that Jesus expected us all to sacrifice ourselves in that cause. Robinson, along with Paul Hoffmann and John S. Kloppenborg, was a leader of the International Q Project. That project worked from 1989 to 1996 to establish the text of Q, and that resulted in the publication of *The Critical Edition of Q*,[3] and then in a popular form: *The Sayings of Jesus: The Sayings Gospel Q in English*.[4]

After the Jesus Seminar completed its work, many of the major figures from the Seminar undertook to write their understanding of what the seminar had demonstrated or proved regarding the nature of that person, Jesus, in that place and time two thousand years ago. They tried to set down a proper picture of Jesus. A somewhat humorous fact came to light as these books by Crossan, Mack, Borg, Robinson, and others began to appear. Each of the members of the Jesus Seminar, who had largely agreed for thirty years on the words in the gospels actually spoken by Jesus, described in their monographs a markedly different Jesus than all the other members of the Jesus Seminar.

They had all looked into the deep well of history to discern who that man from Nazareth really was from that place and that time so long ago, way down there in the historical record. They each saw deep down in that well what you always see when you look down into a deep well. They all saw their own faces reflected from the depths of the well of history. As is inevitable for us humans, each contrived a Jesus made in the image of the scholar himself. That is exactly what Pope Leo X had done. He conceived a Jesus made to fit his political image and objectives. That myth of Jesus had served the church quite well over the centuries, he was sure. Mack thought he was a kind of Roman philosopher called a Cynic, Crossan believed he was a simple peasant, and Robinson says Jesus was a sincere and heroic person, but an unrealistic or impractical ascetic.

---

3. James M. Robinson et al., eds., *The Critical Edition of Q*, Hermeneia Supplements (Minneapolis: Fortress, 2000).

4. James M. Robinson, ed., *The Sayings of Jesus: The Sayings Gospel Q in English*, Facets (Minneapolis: Fortress, 2002).

Marcus Borg, an Episcopal priest, probably comes closest to the truth about that man from that place and that time. He said that what we need to do is not simply distill out of the gospel what were the real words of Jesus. We need to get into the heart of Jesus. He says that when people use the term, Jesus Christ—or Jesus, the Christ—they do not mean to refer simply to that man from that place and that time. Borg asserts that when we confess the words of the Creed or read the text from John's Gospel, what we mean by saying "I believe in Jesus Christ, our Lord," is "I believe in God." We use the name Jesus Christ to mean God, the creator, sustainer, and savior of the entire material world.

In Hebrew Bible tradition (OT), Bible believers knew God by the name, Yahweh. That worked fairly well most of the time, but it lacked personalization. It remained ethereal and abstract. When Christians who do not speak Hebrew undertake to name God, they call him Jesus Christ. For better or worse, Christianity gave tangible personalism to our notion of God. Today we know God by the name Jesus Christ, says Borg. We mean to address God by that name. That personalizes our concept of God as a person in our lives and in history. For us the notions of God and Jesus Christ have coalesced into the same meaning. I think Borg is on to something important there.

When Karl Barth, the greatest Reformed theologian of the twentieth century, ended his life's work he said he could summarize his twenty or more massive volumes of theology by the simple children's song, "Jesus loves me, this I know, for the Bible tells me so." Moreover, when he said that, he meant to be saying, "God loves me, this I know, for the Bible tells me so." He was using that name, Jesus, which just happens to be that man's name from that time and that place, to refer to more than that man from that time and that place. He meant thereby to be calling on God. He was using that name to name God. Marcus Borg would have liked that. He confirms such sentiment by defining Jesus as a man with a life full of God.

Borg suggests that the Creed intends to say in its second article, "If you want to see God the easy route is to see Jesus." When we read or recite John 3:16–17 and confess in the Creed, "I believe in Jesus Christ, God's unique son, our Lord," we mean to say "We believe that God is with us in our lives and in history." Borg says that Jesus was a man from that time and place so long ago, but he was a man with such a life full of God that if we want to see God we must look into the face of Jesus Christ.

His statement is interesting because you can tell that he recognizes that in the end none of us knows exactly how to talk about God. We can only talk in metaphors. We cannot capture God in definitions or theological propositions; but we can name him. We can fill that name with a heart full of our understanding of what God is up to in this world and in our lives and in our time—and what God was up to in the brief moment of that man from Nazareth, and in the meeting between humanity and God in Jesus' three short years of ministry two thousand years ago.

All of us have a deep need for a personalized metaphor to fix in place the story of our faith, the story of our understanding of God; and to stake down the function and role of Jesus in that story in a personalized metaphor. All humans have a deep psychological and spiritual need for a personalized experience of God, a concretized metaphor, a confessional formulation of the truth which can settle the central psycho-spiritual hunger in us for a tangible sense of God's nature and presence with us. "I believe in Jesus Christ, God's son, our Lord" nails down that truth about God that is central to the story. It is that palpable nature and presence of the God of love and grace to which we testify when we say, "I believe in Jesus Christ, God's unique son, our Lord." In the story we have of Jesus, the Christ, we see God present here and now as a tangible part of our human history.

Probably one of the reasons there was such a variety of Judaisms afloat, in the era of the Hebrew Bible and at the time of Jesus, was that it was so difficult to create or find a personalized metaphor. The name Yahweh was an attempt at a personalized metaphor: Yahweh instead of Baal, instead of Dagan, instead of the Asherim. By contrasting the name of Yahweh with the names of all the other gods, believers filled that name with as much content as they could: Covenant God, God of grace and mercy; but then also God as Warrior and threat and terror. The absence of a tangible name for God that satisfies the hunger of the human heart for a personalized metaphor is probably a fatal flaw in any religion. Lacking a palpable personalized image is not quite the same as the ability, for better and for worse, to say, "I know God in Jesus Christ as Savior and Lord."[5]

Judaism never quite got to that point. Judaism tended in the opposite direction, psychologically, by avoiding the use of the name of God

---

5. See below my address to Christian idolatrizing of Christology over the centuries, a fatal flaw in historic Christianity.

altogether, in order to emphasize and protect the transcendental sacred character of God's name. I suppose that is why the Epistle to the Hebrews starts out with those amazing verses, "God, who in bits and pieces, at various times in the past (now and then), spoke to us through the prophets, has in these last days visited us in his Son."

Some years ago I had a graduate student at the University of Michigan, in the Department of Near Eastern Studies, who wanted to write a master's thesis on why Christianity survived and triumphed over all the competing religions in the ancient world in the first three or four centuries of our era. In those centuries there was, after all, quite a lot of competition between the old Roman religion, the imperial cult, the numerous mystery religions that were very popular, Mithraism—which was a Persian religion with a redemptive blood sacrifice quite similar to Christianity, and then there were many kinds of Judaisms, and there was Christianity.

All of these were competing for the mind and the heart of the people of the Mediterranean basin. My student wanted to study why it was that Christianity survived as the triumphant religion. I thought this study was a good idea. I did not know in what direction he could possibly take this research. I was delighted when, in the end, adducing a lot of significant data, he said that he believed that the reason that Christianity survived and dominated the scene was psychological, namely, because it was the only religion that offered a story about God personally visiting us. Well that is what the Epistle to the Hebrews claimed, of course. That is the story that was necessary to fill our essential psychological and spiritual hunger. We needed that story to fill our need for a personalized, tangible, metaphor about a palpable person in whom God is present to us. Because of the presence to us of the tangible person of Jesus, the Christ, we can understand the story of God in God's personal relationship with us.

Marcus Borg was on the right track. When we look down the deep well of history, through the lens of the creed, we do not see our own reflection at the bottom of the well. We do not create God present to us in Jesus in our own image. The Creed encapsulated the essence of the story, the essence of God's story with humanity, in one simple line, "I believe in God the father, almighty, maker of heaven and earth; and in Jesus Christ, God's unique Son, our Lord." Therein the creed claims that God has visited us in his Son and that makes all the difference in the world for the likes of us. In that biblical claim we can see the composite image of the human community's experience of seeing God present to us. Looking at that man in history we can see our communal human psycho-spiritual face reflected in his face. It is reflected in terms of the fulfillment of our perceived hunger for a tangible connection with God. So Paul could say so confidently, "God was in Christ . . ." (2 Corinthians 5:19).

I believe in Jesus Christ, God's unique son, our Lord!

3

Conceived of the Spirit, Born of a Virgin

It was thoroughly predictable that from early in the Jesus Movement nothing in the entire spectrum of Christian ideas or doctrines caused more conflict, across the whole breadth of the church, than this line in the Creed: the claim of some Christians, that Jesus was born of a virgin. Nothing has caused so much dissention and conflict in the Christian community ever since, as has this unusual idea. It virtually split the church from the very beginning. The Jerusalem Church, dominated by Jesus own family, held that there was no such thing as the virgin birth of Jesus. That church seems eventually to have influenced the thought and perspective of the Church of Palestine and Syria, which held out long and vigorously for a human Jesus whose value to us was in his being a Great Teacher.

On the other hand, the Church centered in Alexandria, Egypt and in Rome held out for the virgin birth of Jesus. Their opponents believed this was because they wanted to give a more supernatural dimension to the ideology of the Christian faith. This became the source and occasion for much debate during the formation of the Apostles' Creed. The Alexandrian Bishop and his retinue won the battle and so we have this line in the creed which declares, "I believe in Jesus Christ . . . conceived of the Holy Spirit, born of the virgin Mary."

The Jewish opponents of Christianity in the first two centuries fixed upon this conflict and made much of the New Testament references to Jesus as the son of Joseph, the carpenter, and upon the genealogies in the gospels which trace Jesus' lineage through Joseph, rather than through Mary (Matthew 1:1–17; Luke 3:23–38). This conformed to the perspective of the Jerusalem Church led by Jesus' brother, James, as well as to the outlook of the Ebionites, and the viewpoint of the Syrian Church. Moreover, the legend afloat since that time claimed that Jesus was conceived in Mary by a Roman soldier. We know from the earliest icons that Jesus looked like a Roman and not a Jew. He was tall, angular, had a rust colored beard and long straight hair. He looked more north European than Mediterranean.

There is no good reason to believe that Jesus was born of a virgin. Paul, who wrote the earliest books in the New Testament, says nothing about Jesus' birth in any of his numerous epistles, though in Philippians 2 and Colossians 1 he makes much of Jesus having come from God to reveal the mysteries of God to us. If he knew Jesus had had a magical or supernatural birth, he surely would have used that as ammunition to support his exalted Christology of Jesus as a heavenly being.

Of all the four gospels, moreover, only two have a birth narrative. Mark, the first to be written, has no reference to his origin at all. John, the last to be written in its present form, also has no reference to any birth story and starts right out from the beginning making Jesus divine: the Logos or self-expression of God, sent to earth to become human in the man, Jesus. Had John known of a virgin birth, he would have explained that it was in such a manner, and by such extraordinary means, that the *Logos* got into the man, Jesus of Nazareth. He is silent on it and represents a Jewish Christian perspective at the end of the first or beginning of the second century. John's perspective is very much like Paul's outlook four or five decades earlier.

Only Luke and Matthew have birth stories for Jesus. Luke was Mary's physician in her old age in Ephesus. Undoubtedly, the fact that he knows so much detail about the birth story, and other personal information about Jesus, is a result of his close acquaintance with Mary. She would surely have told him all she knew. However, while Luke has a birth narrative for Jesus, he has no virgin birth. He indicates that the angel appeared to Mary while she was a virgin, but he does not say that the conception was supernatural or that Jesus was conceived or born while she was still a virgin. Mary would have known. She had a firsthand account. She was an eyewitness! The story is told by Luke as if Joseph and Mary were having a baby and he was born while they are on a trip to Bethlehem. Of course, the story suggests that this was "of God," but then, so were the conceptions of my seven kids. They were prompted and inspired by the Holy Spirit! Children are a heritage of the Lord.

That leaves only the birth narrative in Matthew's gospel, probably written a decade or two after that of Luke. There we have a specific declaration that Jesus was born of a virgin, and the author quotes an Old Testament prophecy to prove it. Unfortunately, he quotes the prophecy incorrectly. Isaiah 7:14 declares that a young maiden, that is, an unmarried woman, shall conceive and bear a son and they shall call his name Immanuel, which means in Hebrew, "God is with us!" It would not have been extraordinary for an unmarried woman to conceive a child, since in Old Testament ethics betrothed couples were expected to have a full-fledged sexual life so that it could be determined that the woman could get pregnant. If she could not the marriage could be nullified. If she could the marriage could go forward. The Septuagint translated the Hebrew word for unmarried young maiden, in Isaiah 7:14, by using the Greek term *parthenos*. This Greek word normally means approximately the same thing as the Hebrew word it translates, i.e., young unmarried maiden, not necessarily a virgin. However, in special contexts *parthenos* can indicate virginity. Obviously Isaiah did not mean to indicate virginity. Had he so intended, he would have been more precise about that and not used a term that normally did not mean virgin.

When Matthew wrote his gospel he spelled out *his interpretation* in his quotation of Isaiah 7:14 and declared that the prophet had claimed that "a *virgin* shall conceive and bear a son, and his name shall be called Emmanuel." Obviously, Matthew had a special investment in casting Jesus' origins in a miraculous scene. This was a way to account for what he saw as Jesus' uniqueness. It is obvious throughout Matthew's gospel that the author writes that gospel to prove that Jesus is the promised Messiah of the Hebrew Bible; the one who had come to reveal the mysteries of God to us. Matthew alludes to Hebrew Bible quotations whenever he can do so conveniently. He does it in order to prove a point he is making about Jesus special nature. Matthew's Jesus fulfills all the messianic prophecies of the Hebrew Bible or Old Testament.

What the author seems to have overlooked is the fact that God does not need to perform a miracle in order to be present to us in God's unique son, our Lord. God can accomplish that objective by any means God chooses, of course, by sexual intercourse or virgin birth. Heroic stories of extraordinary conception and birth tend to supernaturalize the nature of the person involved. Surely Jesus' very nature would have left his witnesses reaching for extraordinary ways of accounting for him. So we have Matthew's surprising, unique, and groundless, story.

That kind of storytelling was common in the ancient world. Such stories were told of historical and mythic characters like Alexander the Great, Hercules, Pythagoras, and numerous other Greek and Roman heroes of myth, legend, and history. Frequently the stories reported that Zeus or Jupiter conceived boy children on young human maidens or virgins and they turned out to be "Sons of God," that is, heroic and supernaturally accomplished figures.

One can easily see why such things would be said of figures such as Alexander, Hercules, and Pythagoras. These divinizing stories were designed to account for the extraordinary qualities, characters, and accomplishments of such men. Matthew seems to have adopted that literary mode of his time to account for Jesus extraordinary qualities and accomplishments, quoting ancient prophecy to reinforce his point, and giving it as heroic and supernatural a cast as possible.

As indicated above, Pope Pius IX promulgated the doctrine of Mary's immaculate conception. When he set forth that doctrine he was not dealing with Mary's virginal conception of Jesus. He went one step further and claimed that Mary, herself, was immaculately conceived by her mother, that is, without sexual intercourse. This seemed important to him to account for the heroic character and achievement of Mary in virginally bearing Jesus. Pius IX went a step further in this mythologizing. He claimed that Mary, at the end of her life, was bodily carried up to heaven, her body and soul being immediately reunited in her transcendent abode. It is referred to as the doctrine of the Assumption of Mary. Those medieval myths, promulgated by the Pope, mainly for political and propaganda reasons, were probably about on a par with Matthew's mistranslating Isaiah 7:14 for his special purposes. There is no good reason to believe in a virgin birth of Jesus Christ, despite its presence in the Apostles' Creed and the Gospel of Matthew.

On the other hand, there is no question about Jesus being conceived by the Spirit. We know from his words and work that he was "of the Spirit." That does not need to be miraculous. Most things from God are ordinary and not supernatural: creation, providence, beauty, and grace are all present to us in every-day and unspectacular kinds of human experiences. God normally seems to work through the ordinary modes he has set in motion in this world of his. The important thing about Jesus is that he is "of the Spirit" and so he is Immanuel, God with us! The creed is soundly at the center in that claim. He is a man with a life full of God.

You can tell that by the way he spoke and behaved. How true it is that a young maiden conceived and bore a child and his truly proper name is Immanuel, God with us!

The most interesting thing about the claim of the virgin birth in Matthew's gospel is the fact that it is never again mentioned, noted, or referred to in scripture. No doctrine, teaching, argument, or line of thought, in the entire Bible, is hung on the claim of Mary's virginity! It seems to be just a non-fact in the whole Bible—irrelevant. The story is told and then forever ignored until the Bible is completed. Even in the Apostles' Creed, where it is clearly stated that Jesus was born of the *virgin* Mary, no Christian truth is attached to it or depends upon it. It has nothing further to do with any of the rest of the creed.

Of course, there were later attempts to hang some doctrines upon this claim of Jesus' supposed immaculate conception. Pius IX was not the only one to make something of this erroneous myth. The writers of the Heidelberg Catechism, a creedal document in the Reformed tradition, argued in the sixteenth century that Jesus needed to be born of a virgin so that he could be truly pure and, therefore, able to be our pristine and holy savior, altogether without and unconnected to sin. This foolish notion, of course, is unbiblical. It implies that there is something inherently impure about sex and that anyone associated with it is defiled, sinful, and cannot be God's anointed. This erroneous attitude in the church toward sex has done a lot of damage.[1]

The Heidelberg Catechism does not go quite so far as Pius IX. It does not remove sex two generations from Jesus just to make sure. It simply takes Matthew's erroneous interpretation of the LXX translation of the Hebrew word for young and unmarried maiden and tries to make Jesus heroically godly, as though his being "of the Spirit" was not enough to account for his uniqueness. Matthew, the Heidelberg Catechism, and Pius IX are simply wrong. There was no virgin birth. Jesus was conceived and born in the normal way, and that is what makes him so spectacular as the man with a life full of the holy and divine Spirit. No wonder he became the watershed and turning point of history.

On the one hand, nothing is hung on his being born of a virgin, but on the other hand, everything is hung upon his being "conceived by the Spirit." Isaiah was right: Emmanuel, God is with us in a unique way in

---

1. See J. Harold Ellens, *Sex in the Bible, A New Consideration* (Westport, CT: Praeger, 2006).

Jesus of Nazareth! John picked up on this and without fooling around with myths of a virgin birth, he declared outright that Jesus Christ carried within him God's nature and self-expression in the form of God's *Logos*. Paul celebrates the same quality in Jesus, describing him as being "of the Spirit."

In Philippians 2:3–11 Paul describes Jesus as having been in the form and nature of God. Deciding not to hang on to that divine immunity, Jesus emptied himself of all his divine prerogatives, and became a man born of a woman, born under the law, that he might redeem us who are under the law. Paul's term for woman in this case specifically refers to a mature woman and intentionally avoids any reference to virginity. Again, in Colossians 1 Paul declares that Jesus contained the full nature of the Godhead, bodily, which John reflects in his gospel at 1:14, "The *Logos* was made flesh and dwelt among us, and we beheld his glory, glory as of the uniquely begotten of the Father, full of grace and truth."

What counts is the creed's declaration that he came from or carried in him the Spirit (*Chokmah, Wisdom, Logos, Sophia*) of God. This made him the unique Son of Man, as he called himself, the revealer of the mysteries of God, and our savior. If one wants to spend a lifetime in Bible study it is a good idea to pursue the question of what *that* means, the unique Son of Man, rather than spending any energy on figuring out the virgin birth.

We must always read the creed with an eye open to what the bishops were trying to nail down. We should not become preoccupied with the language they used to do it. If, "in the Spirit," we read of his being "of the Spirit," no further mythology is necessary. It does not take a rocket scientist to understand that. He was a man with a life full of the Spirit and the only proof we need is that, as we connect with God through him, he fills our lives with that Holy Spirit.

4

Suffered, Died, Buried

The fourth issue taken up by the Creed is expressed in the line, I believe in Jesus Christ who "suffered under Pontius Pilate, was crucified, died, and was buried." The surprise in this line is the emphasis the creed gives to the deadliness of Jesus life. He was crucified. His death was real. He was buried for sure!

Pontius Pilate has been known to everyone in the Western world for 2000 years. He might easily have been completely overlooked by history. His assignment in Judea was just another relatively minor post in the grand Roman Empire. But he became famous by being infinitely infamous. He has been known for two millennia as the executioner of God! What a way to be remembered! Professor Paul Maier, from Western Michigan University, wrote a book thirty years ago titled *Pontius Pilate*.[1] It is an historical novel about the life of Pilate.

In that book he has a nearly hilarious scene in which a newspaper reporter interviews Pilate in his old age, in retirement at Pompeii in Italy. The reporter asks him about the occasion, now long past, when he had on trial before him this fellow, Jesus of Nazareth. Pilate scratches his head and thinks a while and then says he can not rightly recall the situation or the name. "There were lots of Jews named Jesus, you know, and that assignment always involved a lot of insurrectionists and revolutionaries." He simply did not remember that story. He could not remember the man or the occasion. He said he would have to look it up in the records. Pilate would not be remembered today if it had not been for his encounter with Jesus; a fateful encounter that made him famous by making him infamous.

---

1. Paul L. Maier, *Pontius Pilate, A Biographical Novel* (Garden City, NY: Doubleday, 1968).

It is interesting that the bishops who wrote the Apostles' Creed should have gone to such trouble to record that it was Pilate who had caused Jesus' suffering and who had crucified him. I suspect that the reason the creed emphasizes this so strongly lies in the fact that its authors were trying to walk a long way around anything that would smell of anti-Semitism, any suggestion that it was the Jews who killed Christ. That is interesting in the face of the fact that the gospels clearly claim that it was the leaders of the Jewish community who forced Pilate's hand, and declared, "His blood be upon us and upon our children."

Moreover, despite this careful guard against it by the creed, throughout the Middle Ages and on into the Modern Era Christians have rather consistently accused the Jews of deicide—of killing God. This has been so strong and pervasive a claim, and so great an offense to the Jewish Community, that Pope John XXIII publicly apologized for the millennia of this Christian abuse of Jews. He was surely right in doing so, and directly in line with the Apostles' Creed. Obviously the bishops who wrote the creed tried hard to get around the abusive sentiment of anti-Semitism. Pilate is made the fall guy in the creed because of the desire to intentionally avoid that awful charge against the Jewish people that is made so clearly in the New Testament gospels. The bishops tried to set this sensitive matter on the right road, right from the beginning.

He was crucified, dead, and buried! The stark reality of those words is intended to inform us that this was not just a set-up in the creed for the drama of resurrection. The creed wants us to know that he endured hellish agony. That is what the creed wants to say: tragedy, horror! It is easy for us to slip past this agony, easy to rush over Good Friday, easy to hurry on to Easter morning, and take lightly the intervening darkness and death. It is easy to cover Good Friday with the frosting of Easter's sweet light.

This is not just some drama designed to set the resurrection in a theatrical light. The creed wants us to know that Jesus' hellish agony was real and his special connection with God and god-ness did not immunize him from this anguish. It was devastatingly real for him. The only worse suffering than crucifixion is being burned at the stake; and if you are burned at the stake, they tell me, the agony only lasts ten minutes. Crucifixion can last for ten hours until you drown in your own body fluids, which collect and coagulate in your pericardium, pleural cavity, and lungs, choking you to death. He was crucified, dead, and buried.

Are we really able to hear that today? Can we really internalize, as our genuine experience, what that felt like to him? He suffered and died! Jesus died! God died? That is the word of the creed here. It wants us to hear that kind of gospel. No wonder that old hymn wrenches our hearts so strongly:

> Were you there when they crucified my Lord?
> Were you there when they nailed him to the tree?
> Were you there when they laid him in the tomb?
> Oh, Oh, Sometimes it causes me to tremble!
> Were you there when they laid him in the tomb?

He learned obedience through suffering, the Bible says in the Epistle to the Hebrews, and so became worthy to be our savior. He went through an ordeal just like ours, that same epistle asserts—yet without sin. He did it right. He did not fail. He did not sin: did not fall short of the mark; did not shrink from the ultimate cost; did not let the burden and the trauma distract him from his authentic commitments—from his calling, from his true self.

Jesus died! God died? Somebody laid hold of the horns of death and wrestled that monster to the ground—to a hole in the ground; and there, "six feet of earth made us all the same size." Even Jesus! Even God?

He died! For you? For me? Try to love as he loved and you will pay a price as stark and costly. Can we do that? They stuck him in the ground, in a hole in the ground! He was buried, says the creed! That's final. That certifies it! He was dead as a door nail! No mere drama—no make believe—no mother goose story from some ethereal world! No divine escape—no quick easy slide to Easter morning! D-E-A-D—dead!

John, the apostle whom Jesus loved, stood there at the cross, and through that lens of the deadliness of Jesus' death, John saw the truth. We hear its echoes in the last chapters of the Apocalypse of Saint John. We usually call it the Book of Revelations; there in chapter 21:1–4 these awesome words sound forth:

> I heard a great voice from God's throne.
> "Look, Look," said the voice,
> "God lives with us—and dies with us!
> He is our God and we are his people!
> God himself is with us!
> God will wipe away every tear from our eyes.
> Death shall be no more!

Nor shall there be mourning, nor crying,
nor pain anymore.
These things are passing away!"

5

He Descended into Hell

WE HAVE COME TO the most enigmatic passage in the Confession of our faith. "I believe in Jesus Christ . . . he descended into hell." Most Christians read or recite this line in the creed with a large sense of mystification. Many of us read it with disbelief, and some of us with disgust. Neither theologians nor congregants in our churches have ever known what to do with this strange line, and so we tend to keep silent at this place, while reciting the creed; or we recite it while dissociating from its meaning, just mouthing the words, mumbling our way through.

That is a sign of spiritual health because this line is a lie. Jesus did not descend into hell. To confess that he descended into hell is to affirm a falsehood. It never happened. It has no meaning. It is an offensive mistake by the bishops of the ancient church councils. We know this line in the creed is an untruth for a number of reasons. First of all and most important, it is unbiblical. There is no place in the Bible where this notion is taught. Second, no other element of Christian faith or understanding is related to or hung upon this claim in the creed. Third, there is no such place, thing, or experience as an afterlife in hell.

In the entire OT there is no developed concept of an afterlife of any kind. The OT refers to the dead as going to *sheol*, a Hebrew word for the underworld, with approximately the same import as that concept of the underworld in the ancient Mesopotamian, Egyptian, and Greek mythologies. That underworld in all those cultures was a place of the dead, a place of some kind of ghostly existence that was not differentiated as one place for the good guys and one for the bad ones. There is no concept of hell in the OT.

Some OT believers, like David, prayed that God would not leave them in Sheol but would find a place for them closer to God's heart, and imbued with real life in eternity. However, they had no notion of the truth of such a possibility, only a whimsical hope that it might be the case. Akhenaton (Ikhnaton), the monotheist Pharaoh of Egypt before the time of Moses, also prayed such a longing prayer, but people in those cultures did not count on such a heavenly possibility. They only knew of an undifferentiated Sheol.

When the OT was translated into Greek, the Hebrew word, Sheol, was translated into the Greek word, Hades, the term for underworld in Homer's *Iliad* and *Odyssey*. When the King James Version (KJV) of the Bible was published, the translators in 1611 CE translated Hades as hell, and gave it a moral interpretation as the place where the wicked go for punishment. That was an error. It is not biblical.

Of course, the New Testament, in the KJV, refers to hell also, and carries that moral overtone with it. However, the original Greek of the NT has the term Hades. Moreover, Jesus refers to the wicked as going into Gehenna, outer darkness, and the place of the goats rather than the sheep. But Jesus, as the incarnate human that he was, spoke in terms of the language and metaphors of his time. He even refers once to someone going to Hades and not having any chance to get out of there. However, he does not speak of hell, and he does not refer to Hades as an eternal place of punishment of the wicked. For him it is merely the Sheol of the OT, the shadowy underworld where all the dead are warehoused, so to speak. Moreover, Gehenna meant the city dump outside the southeast corner of the wall of Jerusalem, where "the worms never die and the fire is never quenched," as in any city dump.

When Jesus spoke of death, he always referred to it as going to be with his Father, or in Paul's terms, "going to be with the Lord." In this he definitely referred to a substantive state of blessedness after death; and Paul refers to it as a continuation of the eternal life on God's plain that we begin here already as believers. However, when Jesus refers to the sheep and the goats, the outer darkness, and the symbolic Gehenna of suffering, he is never referring to a substantive place or state of existence out there, after death. He is always referring to a contingent situation, namely, the state of meaningless or suffering any person has who is separated from God. That condition of hellishness is what we experience here and now, in our sense of alienation from God, and, therefore, alienation from our true and whole selves.

So how did the ancient bishops get away with inserting this line in the creed, and why did they do it? Let us start with the latter point.

Obviously, there could be only one reason to insert it and that was to scare the hell out of everybody. That is, to intimidate the general populace of the church and thereby enhance the power of the bishops and the official church. It kept the natives in line, they thought. Fear of hell was good for their souls. Moreover, it tended to increase the money in the collection plate and the inheritances left to the church in the wills of the dying.

But where did the bishops get this notion about Jesus descending into hell, and with what authority did they get away with inserting this unbiblical and scandalous line into the creed. Well, they claimed that they got it from the Bible. They referred to 1 Peter 3:18–20a. It says there that when Jesus died he went to visit the spirits in bondage who had not listened to God's warning in the days of Noah. The passage specifically declares that Jesus went to the place of the dead, i.e., the underworld, in the Greek sense of that term. The text at this place does not refer to Sheol, Hades, or hell. It refers to visiting the "spirits in prison, who did not formerly obey, in the days of Noah."

Obviously, a number of interesting things are going on in this passage. First, it says Jesus went to visit the spirits in prison. Second, it says these were the spirits who did not obey when Noah obeyed and got into the ark. Third, it means that these spirits were those who were killed by the flood. Fourth, in implies that they are imprisoned in the ghost-like existence of the Greek underworld with Agamemnon, Achilles, Hector, and the others who predeceased Jesus. Fifth, it implies that Jesus' visit to them gave them a second chance to restore their real life. Sixth, this means that Peter believed, with Jesus and Paul, that you could escape the ghost-like existence of Sheol, or the underworld, by believing in the ministry of Jesus; so that then death for you would be "going to be with the Lord." That was an improvement over the Greek idea. Seventh, this surely fit with the general notion in Paul, and most of the NT, that God intends to save all humans, in spite of ourselves, and that in the end the entire created world will be renewed and restored for all of us, the good, the bad, and the ugly (Romans 8:18–26).

That is why it is clear that whatever Peter meant with these strange ideas that he got from the apocryphal book of *I Enoch*, it is in no sense the same as what the bishops said in this line in the creed. There is no basis in the Bible for the claim that "He descended into hell." Let us get that straight, once and for all. Peter was trying to solve the problem of how God's universal salvation relates to all those poor folks that died before the coming of Jesus Christ as savior. He was not trying to create a theology of hell, nor was he claiming that Jesus went there. He claimed, as does *I Enoch*, that the Son of Man visited the dead in the place of the dead. In *I Enoch*, the visit of the Son of Man to the dead is to bring judgment upon the disobedient. In Peter's understanding, Jesus' visit is to lift the lost to life, real life, life on God's plain, i.e., what Paul calls the eternal life that starts now in the life of faith and goes on forever in a blessed eternity with God. Peter knew that a God who would consign humans to an everlasting hell would be a monster no one should worship or honor.

So why do we keep saying this line in the Creed, "He descended into hell?" Well, that is easy to answer. We recite the creed, not as a literal statement of contemporary faith, but as an historical document which keeps us, as the church, in touch with our ancient history, good and bad. It is probably a good thing to keep these old historical documents around, like the Apostles' Creed, the Heidelberg Catechism, and the Westminster Confession, though they all have really ridiculous and offensive claims in them. We ought to face that honestly.

The Heidelberger Catechism, for example, says that the worship services of Catholic Christians are "a popish idolatry." Now, that is not nice. Worse, it is unbiblical to say such a nasty thing. It is flat-out untrue and offensive. We know better, but we keep that old rag around because it keeps us aware of the very good and very bad in our Christian and un-Christian history as the church. The first two sections of the Heidelberger are the very best theology ever written. "What is my only comfort in life and in death? That in life and in death, in body and soul, I am not my own but belong to my faithful savior!" So let's hang on to those old historical markers and celebrate what we can in them. However, whenever we recite the Apostles' Creed, let us remember that when we come to the line, "He descended into hell," we should laugh in our hearts at the pretensions of pompous theologians, and the intimidations of manipulative bishops, wherever they may be.

Some Christians seem always inclined to focus on the negatives in any situations. That is psychopathology, not good theology or wholesome spirituality. Let us recite the creed every Sunday concentrating on the positives in it and laughing our way through the ridiculous stuff like virgin births and descents into hell.

I am reminded somewhat of the two old Scots-Presbyterians walking past a rather disheveled and untended cemetery. The perpetually negative one said, "Ain't it a shame that this younger generation has no respect, is lazy and apathetic, and does not care for or tend the memory of the saintly ancestors who have gone before. I would not be buried in a place like that if it killed me." His always positive and optimistic companion said, "Well, my sentiments about it were quite the other way around. I really thought the place was rather quaint and homey. It seems downright picturesque and natural, almost other worldly. I think I would really like to be buried in a quaint old place like that, should I live and be well!"

Obviously it makes quite a difference if you are inclined to always see the darks side of things; of if it is in your nature to concentrate on the light of the divine spirit.

6

He Rose from the Dead

THE SIXTH PROPOSITION OF faith that we find in the Apostles' Creed is the line that most Christians most of the time consider the most important affirmation in the Creed: He arose from the dead. Of course, the notion of Jesus' resurrection has been hotly debated since that first Easter morning. The gospel records tell us that the first people who said that it *could not be true* were the apostles. When Mary and the other women told them that an angel said he had risen from the dead, the eleven disciples thought it was female histrionics and said it could not be true. They continued to disbelieve and despair until they actually saw the risen Christ. The second group that did not believe he had risen was the traditional Jews. They claimed that the disciples had stolen his body out of the grave during the night and had run off with it.

That claim by the general population of Jerusalem is interesting for a lot of reasons. First, that was a possible explanation for the empty tomb. Second, the critics of the Jesus movement would have wanted to propagandize the notion that Jesus had come to nothing. They had, after all, strongly desired to exterminate him and any notion that he had survived somehow would have put fear, anger, and disappointment in their hearts. They would have been asking themselves whether, despite their having gotten the Romans on their side in executing this man from Nazareth, it were possible that Jesus had won the contest after all, and somehow gotten away. Third, they must have been aware of the fact that this scenario of Jesus' resurrection was a kind of replay of what had happened to the messiah figures of the people of the Dead Sea Scrolls, the Qumran Community.

According to Israel Knohl, a scholar of the Dead Sea Scrolls, in 4 BCE, that is, just four decades earlier, in fact about the time Jesus was born, the Royal and the Priestly Messiahs of the Qumran Community, had both been murdered on the streets of Jerusalem, and left there to decay in the hot Palestinian sun.[1] Their disciples were not able to get to the bodies because of the Roman guard that had cordoned off the area. The bodies lay there for three days untended. On the third day they disappeared and the Roman guards as well as the Essenes from Qumran were mystified as to what had happened to them. The Romans thought some disciples had surreptitiously found a way to steal them away. The Essene believers from Qumran concluded that since the Romans did not seem to know what happened, and *they themselves* had not removed the bodies, the only explanation must be that "on the third day they rose from the dead and ascended into heaven." The religious authorities in Jerusalem would not have wanted to see this scenario played out again in Jesus' case, making their actions in doing away with Jesus as shameful as the action of the Romans in killing the two Messiahs from Qumran.

In Peter's sermon on Pentecost, when people from all over the Mediterranean basin were converted to faith in Jesus Christ, Peter clearly had in the back of his mind that old story about the Qumran Messiahs being killed and resurrected and ascending to heaven (Acts 2). He also was well aware of the anxiety reigning in Jerusalem at the very moment he was preaching his Pentecost sermon; anxiety about whether history was repeating itself and what this could possibly mean. He does not hesitate to thrust his verbal sword into the most vulnerable place in the heart of the Jerusalem religious authorities and of the crowds who had yelled at the hesitant Pilate, "Crucify Jesus. Give us Barabbas. Crucify Jesus!"

Luke reports that Peter declared without apology, "Men of Israel, Jesus of Nazareth, a man attested to you by God with mighty works and wonders and signs, which God did through him in your midst—this Jesus . . . you crucified and killed by the hands of lawless men, but God raised him up, having loosed the pangs of death, because death cannot hold him" (Acts 2:22-24).

Well, that is bold and courageous talk, great rhetoric, and a confident, condescending diatribe against the Jewish crowd. Is this not a bit of a surprise, coming from a guy who had betrayed Jesus three times only a month and a half earlier; and then when the women had told him Jesus had risen from the dead, he had declared that it could not be so? Was not this the same guy who was huddled with the other ten disciples

---

1. Israel Knohl, *The Messiah before Jesus: The Suffering Servant of the Dead Sea Scrolls* (Berkeley: University of California Press, 2000).

behind barricaded doors just seven weeks before in the upper room in Jerusalem? What is going on here? What has happened? How can we explain this remarkable change from cowering fear to fanatical courage?

The answer is: *Peter had seen the resurrected Jesus!* The eleven surviving disciples had all seen Jesus. But what had they seen? Not the crucified Jesus who was laid in the grave, of course. Not the dead corpse reawakened. Not the product of a bodily resurrection. To make such a claim would be unbiblical. However, they had seen Jesus, that is, they had seen something which at first they could not recognize; but then eventually when he spoke to them, when he broke bread with them, when he ate a piece of fish with them, and when they saw the stigmata of his wounds, they realized it was he after all.

When Mary saw him in the garden on Easter morning, she did not know who he was. When he appeared to the Emmaus travelers, they did not recognize him. When he entered the upper room where the disciples were hiding, and came in without opening a door or a window, they did not recognize him. When he appeared at the lakeshore at Galilee, they did not recognize him. He had to make some characteristic gesture in each case, or speak some familiar word, before they recognized that it was he. He had to manifest himself to them. They could not just automatically see that it was he.

What had changed Peter from a coward and betrayer to a man of courage and strident Christian oratory? He had seen the Lord! That is, he had seen the "glorified Christ." Now we have no way of knowing what in the world that sentence means. We have no way of understanding what the glorified Christ can possibly be. All we know is that it is something we do not know about, but that the disciples saw. They saw something and eventually recognized that it was Jesus, alive in some mode that made it possible for him to go and come without being constrained by time, space, or materiality. He could enter rooms and leave them—through the walls, so to speak. He could beam himself from place to place, to take a line from *Star Trek*. He could eat food to make a demonstration that he was real and not just a chimera of their imagination, but he did not need food to live. He could be one moment in Jerusalem, and the next show up on the shore of the Sea of Galilee, where he had always gone for vacation.

Both Paul and Peter tried to express what was going on in all this esoteric drama. Both of them declare that Jesus died in the flesh (material body—1 Corinthians 15:44; 1 Peter 3:18), but rose in the spirit (glorified body). Paul then continues to speak at length about Jesus' spiritual body and the spiritual bodies we shall all acquire in our eternal life. These ethereal forms of existence are beyond our understanding and the Bible makes no attempt to help us understand them. It merely informs us of Jesus' expectation, expressed toward the end of the gospels, particularly the Gospel of John, that he would be glorified; and that God would be glorified by Jesus being glorified. Then Paul speaks of Jesus' spiritual and glorified body, after his death, as the reason for us to have hope in a similar resurrection for ourselves.

While we cannot understand what we are talking about when we speak of spiritual or glorified bodies, there are a number of things we can say about Jesus' glorified body, as seen by the disciples after his death. Therefore, there are a number of things we can say about Jesus' resurrected form. First, it was not the corpse from the grave revivified, for then the disciples would have recognized it as soon as they saw it. Second, Jesus had obviously completely overcome the effects of death and was alive on the eternal plain. Third, he was not limited or constrained by time or space. Fourth, he was not material in the sense we think of that here and now, for he required no food or drink and he could move about without being restricted or obstructed by material structures. He entered rooms by just appearing there, without accessing the room through doors or windows or even coming in through the walls, really, as though he was coming from some other place in space and moving into the room. Fifth, apparently Jesus, in his glorified or heavenly form, was able to manifest himself visually or he was able to refuse to do so, whichever he wished. Sixth, when he manifested himself, he had the option of doing it in a manner in which it would be obvious to earthly humans who he was, and he had the option to conceal that identity until the right moment of his choosing.

In all his post-resurrection appearances he initially concealed his true identity. It was important to have the eyes to see him, but it was also necessary for him to reveal himself to human eyes. A further implication of all this is that it will be possible for us to recognize each other in our eternal and glorified state. It will be possible for us to make ourselves known to each other, as he did to the disciples, so that they were able to perceive that it was he. We will know our loved ones and friends, and come to know the whole of God's multitude of the redeemed creation to the extent that we wish to know each other and be known to each other.

When we recite the Apostles' Creed to confess our faith and we come to this line that testifies that "on the third day he arose again from the dead," we are confessing that it is the glorified Christ that we believe the apostles saw with their own eyes after his death. That changed their lives! The people of the first century debated what happened to Jesus' body. We do not know and we do not really care. Probably Joseph of Arimathea removed it from his family tomb and put it in some other grave, which he bought for Jesus. It makes no difference. Probably James Tabor is correct that the stone boxes recently found in Jerusalem really are from the family tomb of Joseph and Mary. The boxes have on them the names of the members of that family, including one box with Jesus' name on it.

That debate about what happened to Jesus body is like the debate about whether we should have ourselves embalmed and buried when we die, or go for cremation. It makes no difference which way our bodies are eventually oxidized and returned to the dust from whence we came. We have no investment in the preservation of this old carcass. What we confess as Christians is that death opens the way for all of us to that glorified state in which we shall be our own real, whole, and true selves once and for all. We will have a new and heavenly body. It will not be subject to disease or aging, decay or death, or subject to the limitations of time or space or materiality. We shall be our true and whole selves.

I have a dear friend, a very important and thoughtful man, an insightful lay theologian. He is now 92 years old. He says that he has had a wonderful life and is happy he can still carry on his important work, but he realizes that he will be dead in a decade. Now, he is in no sense afraid of that. I tell him he is in too much of a hurry, since his mother lived to 102. However, he declares that however that may be, what he resents already is the coming loss of the physicality and sensuality of his body. He says, "I really like the tactile and tangible feel of things and I do not want to give it up. I think death is, in that sense, a lousy deal. I like the aesthetic experience of being physically alive to everything in this world, and I enjoy the rewarding palpable sensations of all of my five senses."

Well, I agree with him. Don't we all! I suppose that is the exact reason why Jesus manifested himself to us in his glorified body, so that the disciples could see, and we can see through their eyes, that even better things await us: no more aches and pains, no more mourning and crying. "God will wipe away every tear from our eyes. There shall be no more sea to tear away loved ones. Wars will stop. And death shall be no more" (Revelation 21:1–4).

When we confess that he rose again the third day from the dead, we know that the ancient bishops who wrote that line in the creed did not know exactly what that meant. They only knew that the disciples had seen something indescribable and indefinable and they wanted to testify to it in the creed. We, who recite this line in the creed every Sunday, know that we have no clear idea what it is that we are saying. However, in the light of that line in the creed as it tries to express that which the disciples saw with their own eyes, and by which they were thoroughly changed, old men like me know that it assures us of what the lovely hymn says:

> Be still my soul, the hour is hastening on
> When we shall be forever with the Lord
> When disappointment, grief, and fear are gone
> Sorrow forgot, love's purest joys restored
> Be still, my soul; when change and tears are past,
> All safe and blessed we shall meet at last.

That may not speak to young people with the tender point of pain and hope at which it speaks to those of us who are beginning to contemplate our final years. But I know what does speak even to young people in all of this. When young people recite that line in the Creed, it undoubtedly awakens in them the cadences of this newer hymn: "Then I shall bow in humble adoration, And there proclaim, 'My God, how great thou art!'"

"I believe in Jesus Christ, God's unique son, . . . he rose from the dead."

7

Ascended and Enthroned Judge

NEXT THE ANCIENT BISHOPS tell us, "he ascended into heaven and is seated on the right hand of God the Father Almighty, from thence he shall come to judge the living and the dead." It does not take a rocket scientist to discern where in Scripture they found the texts to ground this confessional claim. The New Testament has many verses that describe Jesus' heavenly abode, as well as his intended return on the clouds of heaven with all the holy angels, in the power and glory of Almighty God, the Father. Throughout most of the church's history this line in the creed, and the Scriptures that back it up, kept the membership in line for fear of the final judgment.

Read the gospels of Matthew, Mark, and Luke and notice how often Jesus refers to the fact that he will be exalted by God by a heavenly ascent and he will be enthroned in power in heaven. Notice especially how often he makes the claim that he will return at the end of time as God's Judge of the world. That has always been rather scary business for Christians, but there it is, spread throughout those gospels, and as if that were not enough, the final shot is fired from Acts 1:11b. "Why do you stand here looking into heaven. This Jesus who was taken up from you in a cloud into heaven, will come again in the same way as you saw him go into heaven."

Whenever the Scriptures mention the enthronement of Jesus at the right hand of God and his impending return as Judge at the end of history, they refer to him as the Son of Man. It is the Son of Man who suffers at the hands of Caiaphas and Pilate, the Son of Man who dies on the cross, the Son of Man who is glorified by God raising him from the dead and bringing him up to his heavenly glory. Everybody who was anybody at the time of Jesus knew that to be the Son of Man meant that you were God's final Judge who would come from heaven at the end of time.

That event would end history as we know it. The Son of Man as Judge would exterminate all the unrighteous, and gather the righteous into the kingdom of God. This was to start up the new age of the renewed heaven and earth. Matthew, Mark, and Luke-Acts were really sure that this scenario was God's design for things and that it would certainly play out as Jesus had said it would. So the bishops quite confidently put all this into the creed.

In fact, they had Jesus' own apparently sturdy testimony endorsing this way of looking at and expecting things in God's economy. In Mark 9:1; Luke 9:27; and Matthew 16:28 Jesus is reported to have declared that there were those standing around in the crowd to which he was preaching who would not die before the Son of Man returned on the clouds of heaven, with the hosts of angels, to judge the living and the dead. That sounds pretty well nailed down, does it not? The first generations of followers of Jesus thought so, and they sat on the edge of their seats, waiting with bated breath, for the imminent end of the world. That is why Paul, in his *early* epistles, advises people not to get married but simply to invest themselves in God's kingdom which would arrive any minute anyway, before they could get a decent marriage going well, in any case, or build an estate to leave for their families.

This is in line with what Professor James M. Robinson contends about Jesus' vision of the kingdom, in which Jesus suggests that his followers should not try to acquire paying jobs, or try to build a family or an estate, but should simply go around declaring God's blessing and grace to everyone who would receive their witness.[1] When anyone received them they were to enter that home and eat and drink and declare that the kingdom of God had come to that place because the people there had acted in unconditional grace and generosity to the disciples, as God acts to all of us.

Unfortunately, there were two problems with this scenario, which the bishops who formulated the Apostles' Creed conveniently overlooked. Problem number one was the fact that the first generation of Jesus' followers began to die off rather fast during the last three decades of the first century. In fact, within ten years after Mark, Matthew, and Luke were written, the first generation was all dead, except perhaps John; and Jesus had not shown up. The church had a real twist in its tail about

---

1. James M. Robinson, *The Gospel of Jesus* (San Francisco: HarperSanFrancisco, 2006).

how to understand the failure of Jesus to return on the clouds of heaven. They did not know whether they had misunderstood Jesus, or Jesus had lied to them, or Jesus was ignorant of the real story, or Jesus had arrogantly promised to perform these wonders of which he was really incapable.

This caused the church to go through a really difficult psycho-spiritual adjustment, as they began to realize, as the *late* Pauline epistles finally acknowledge, that they were in this business of being the church, for the long-run. Those epistles changed the Pauline tune considerably, suggesting that it is good to marry and it is important to build the church and kingdom in the world. Christians began to develop a theology for an indefinitely delayed return of Christ; and to formulate an ethical system for the Christian community to begin culture-building and nation-building, as it launched itself into the second century.

However, problem number two, which the bishops completely avoided, was the fact that they should have paid more attention to John's gospel, the last one to be written. This gospel arrived in its final form late in the first century or even as late as 120 CE, more than a hundred years after Jesus' birth, and three quarters of a century after his death. John's gospel plays quite a different melody than the strident threats of the Synoptic Gospels: Matthew, Mark, and Luke. John mentions the Son of Man fourteen times. Nearly every time that the author of the Fourth Gospel mentions him, it is in a setting in which he is to be glorified by being enthroned in heaven and exalted by God the Father, the Almighty. It is clear enough, at each of these passages about the Son of Man in John, that the author recognizes that most everyone thinks of the Son of Man as the final Judge.

The Gospel of John declares that such an expectation is understandable, but that it is completely wrong-headed. In John 5:27 the gospel declares that God has given Jesus Christ the power and authority to be the Judge, *because he is the Son of Man*. What the bishops overlooked, however, is the fact that every time John's gospel refers to the Son of Man, it tells us that Jesus denied that he was going to act as the Judge. Of course, all the people standing around were thinking, "Oh my! Here is the Son of Man, the agent of the Judgment Day! Woe is me!" Now if you can keep that threat level fairly high you can pretty much keep the natives quiet. But every time the Gospel of John mentions the Son of Man with the implication of judgment, it follows that suggestion of threat with a long monologue in the mouth of Jesus declaring that he will not exercise his power as Judge, he will not act as Prosecutor, there will be no Day of Judgment, and he is not the Judge but the Savior. There is no final judgment, no second coming, and no cataclysm, no end of history in John.

It is true that John 5:27 declares that Jesus is the Judge, but from that verse on for twenty verses, until John 5:47, Jesus makes a big point of declaring that he is not going to witness against anyone or judge anyone. He is not going to tattle about anyone to his father, and God is not going to judge anyone. He insists that he has come into the world to save the whole world. People judge themselves in terms of the posture they hold toward that saving presence of the Son of Man in the world (John 3:13–18).

John's gospel teaches that the judgment has already happened. God carried out the judgment before time began. Before God created the world, according to the Fourth Gospel, God judged the world; and his judgment was that he would save everybody in the world, "For God so loved the world that he gave his unique Son, the Son of Man, that whosoever believes on him shall not perish but have everlasting life; for God sent not his son into the world to condemn the world, but that the *world* through him shall be saved" (John 3:16–17).

If the bishops had paid proper attention to the Gospel of John, they would have been prevented from putting this line in the creed. This line in the creed, like the lines about the virgin birth and the descent into hell, is a lie perpetrated upon the church by its authorities; perpetrated upon faithful devoted people by uninformed or irresponsible and manipulative bishops. It is a false picture of what was going to happen and of what is going to happen in the world.

Of course, if they had not put it into the creed, that would have spoiled all their own fun in threatening church members into good comportment. Fewer would have been driven by guilt and fear to the confessional. Fewer would have come to worship regularly because they thought they had to do so in order to escape divine judgment. Fewer would have come to see the church and the gospel as a kind of fire insurance policy. Of course, less money would have made it to the collection basket out of fear of God's Judgment. The power of the bishops and the church would have been undercut rather badly.

What the bishops should have realized, however, is that if they had not held this threat of divine judgment over the heads of humankind throughout the last twenty centuries, people would have had very positive reasons to go to the confessional. People would have delighted to worship God in spirit and in truth. Christians would have spent their treasure generously on the work of the church and kingdom because they liked the idea and the experience, and they wanted to do so. Threat religion is always sick religion and it is always in the process of getting sicker, because fear feeds on itself. Healthy religion and spirituality has exactly the opposite motivation, and joy inspires joy. Such positive personal spirituality and institutional religion is psychologically and spiritually 180 degrees opposite from the religion of the manipulative and intimidating bishops and their creed.

Healthy religion is a spirituality of freedom to be God's people, *or not to be*. This offers the option of joyful devotion to God because we want to be God's people, *or the option to say, "No!" to God*. Surely, everybody knows that if you cannot say "No!" it means nothing to say "Yes." Healthy devotees of God are always urgently excited about meaningful worship, useful kingdom work, and happy fellowship in the community of faith. Such optimistic members in the church are containers and conveyors of the Holy Spirit of God. We do not do missions because we want to save the pagans' bloody souls from hell. Christians who know the reality and relief of grace are urgently interested in missions in which to share, right now, the reality, relief, and freedom of God's forgiving grace with others who live in spiritualities of threat and fear and shame and guilt.

People who always see the threat side of things are psycho-spiritually sick. Some make themselves always busy with church projects because they think it is their burden and duty to please God. They are usually sure that things are going to fail. They have the kind of sickness the bishops' perspective creates. Being a Christian is not the business of compulsion or burden, but of freedom and fun. If it is not, it is not authentic. It is not of the Spirit. In healthy churches virtually every undertaking is directly related to a specific outcome that is a sizeable blessing to specific human beings in need of mercy, health, education, fellowship, and the inspiration of the Spirit.

The ancient bishops seem to have really believed that the reason to be a Christian is to avoid the terrors of the last Judgment and eternal fires of hell. The truth, however, is that to be a Christian is not an obligation but an opportunity, not a burden but a benefit, not a command to be labored under but an invitation to be seized and celebrated. The reason to be a Christian is because it is more fun to live one's life in the freedom of God's unconditional, radical, and universal grace, than to live in the false fear that is blind to and neglects God's grace, acceptance, and forgiveness.

There are Bible students who are going to be disappointed that there is never going to be a second coming of Christ. There is never going to be a final judgment. There is never going to be a Judgment Day. Popular authors such as Tim LaHaye, who seduce millions with their false prophecies about the rapture, about being *left behind*, and about the coming cataclysmic end of the world, are in for an enormous disappointment and a phenomenal surprise. Their disappointment will be the same as that of the early church when Jesus failed to return, the same as that of the bishops who created sick religion out of selective, threatening passages from the Synoptic Gospels; the same disappointment that all false prophets have experienced when they predicted dramatic divine interventions that still had not happened when those poor fools were enclosed in their coffins.

Many evangelical and fundamentalist Christians today are Zionists. That is, they support the State of Israel with enthusiasm and lots of money. Christian Zionists do this because they believe that the more they do so, the sooner they will provoke the ultimate conflict between Israel and Islam. They think this will hurry along the ultimate cataclysm of the Battle of Har-Megiddo, which will destroy the world as we know it, exterminate all Israelites who do not convert to Christianity, and bring in Christ's Second Coming as the Judge of the living and the dead. They think this will produce a thousand years of blessed Christian rule, in which all the unrighteous and unbelievers will have been exterminated. Such evangelicals and fundamentalists are gleefully spouting this harangue on American TV channels every day and night now. They are in for a serious disappointment. There will be no second coming, no end to history, and no Judgment Day. The Greeks were undoubtedly correct in their scientific assessment that the created world will last forever.

Why some Israelis are willing to be in the same bed with such Christian Zionists is beyond me. Christian Zionists' theology hopes for the extermination of Israel or the conversion of all Jews to Christianity.

However, the bishops of old, the Zionists, all such sensational writers such as LaHaye, and all the legalistic Christians of today, are in for a great surprise; a wonderful, joyful surprise! They are going to be among the crowd of all humanity, to whom the Bible promises that in their moment of transition from time to eternity, "every eye shall see God, every knee shall bow before him as Lord and savior, and every tongue shall confess, as did Thomas, 'My Lord and my God!,' to the glory of God the Father."

No one will be coerced to this faith, of course. It will simply be the case that in view of the evidence, no one will want to disbelieve. We will all want to affirm that beatifying vision. In translation that means that all will see that God is not in the business of judging anyone and is in the business of saving every one, and that is all there is to it. The day of judgment, for each of us, is the moment each of us dies and goes to be with the Lord. The judgment for all human kind will be the same, without exception, "Enter, thou, into the joy of thy Lord!"

Anyone who is disappointed in that has a sick spirituality, informed by bad theology, probably, in part, from the Apostles' Creed. Such folk just do not "get it!" Paul assures us repeatedly, however, that they will get it in the end. Their eyes shall see, knees bow, tongues confess . . . Thanks be to God, the God of utter grace. Anyone who is relieved, and joyfully optimistic, about anticipating that universal salvation by God's grace, has a healthy biblical spirituality, informed by trust in God's unconditional grace. That is of God. That is of God's Holy Spirit.

8

Holy Spirit

Universal Church, Saintly Communion, Fellowship of Forgiveness

As you know by now, I have a lot of hesitation about affirming a lot of the articles of the creed just as they stand; and I am more than ambivalent about at least three of them. I simply do not believe the lines about the virgin birth, the descent into hell, and the second coming of Christ in judgment—because they are unbiblical. If there is one line in the creed that I affirm joyfully and with complete confidence and certainty, however, it is the article which begins the third major section. "I believe in the Holy Spirit: the holy universal Church, the communion of saints, the forgiveness of sins." I believe in the Holy Spirit because I experience the Holy Spirit of God: 1) in my tangible relish of daily life; 2) in some special occasions of God's manifestation to me; and 3) in the life of the holy catholic church: the communion of the saints and the forgiveness of sins.

In his last days on earth, Jesus is reported to have assembled his disciples and informed them straight out, "I am going away. You cannot come along now. I will prepare a place for you and call you later. I will not leave you orphaned. God will send you his Holy Spirit. The Spirit shall lead you into all the truth and bear witness regarding me." Jesus was trying to get out the message that the age of Jesus Christ, as the manifestation of God among humankind, was at an end. The age of the Holy Spirit, as the manifestation of God to us, was about to begin. The disciples were absolutely sure when the church was born on Pentecost, that God had manifested in the world as Holy Spirit and that, thus, Jesus' promise was fulfilled. That did not mean that the Holy Spirit was not present in the world before Pentecost, nor did it mean that the impact of Jesus' incarnation of God in history would no longer be evident.

Never a truer word was spoken, however, than this tenth article of the Apostles Creed. There is a sense in which, if we take this line in the creed seriously, it reveals to us what the entire creed is supposed to be about. It is about how God is present to us in the world, in history, and always has been. The ancient bishops who formulated the creed had a great debate and sturdy difference of opinion about whether the creed should say that God is three individual *persons*, who visit us in various ways at various times; or that God shows up in history in three different and distinctive *modes*. The controversy was known as the debate between the Modalist and the Personalist theories of God's nature and self-revelation in history. In the end the Personalists won out, by some manipulation of the politics of the situation, and so we have the intense struggle in the Apostles' Creed, the Nicene Creed, and the Athanasian Creed, regarding how to describe the three persons without losing monotheism.

In the end, the Personalist theory that prevailed created, in effect, a polytheism. The creed sounds like it speaks of three divine beings: a Father-creator, a Son-savior, and a Holy Spirit-guide and leader of the church. The bishops worked hard to overcome this polytheism in the language of the creed, but they never completely succeeded, except to formulate the questionable conundrum that God is three persons in one being—a notion that never settled it for anyone. It is a tautology, an ambiguous statement, at best. It seems to make foolishness out of plain language.

The Bible knows nothing of a trinity of persons. The Bible knows only of the one true and living God who shows up in human history and in the history of the created world in three *modes*. When we see the grandeur and mindfulness of creation, we think of God in God's fatherliness, siring and thus creating, the world by the ingenuity of evolution, like the gestation of a fetus and the birth of a child. When we see Jesus of Nazareth on the pages of the gospels and read his story, we realize his incredible relevance to the human predicament. We sense the way in which he made God real and tangible to us. We think of God as the son, a brother and a rescuer for us from our mystification over our morality and mortality; savior for us from our endogenous anxiety, fear, guilt, and shame. When we watch how God continues to work in his world through the church, we know, as did the early Christians, that the end of Jesus' life did not end the story of his work in the world, nor his presence in the world, nor God's life in the world. It did not end his story because it did not end our story with God. In this we know and experience God as the Spirit whom Christ promised, the Spirit of Jesus Christ, God's Holy Spirit.

Once we get past all the formalistic and formulaic language of the creed and let it speak to us simply about God, it is clear that the Personalist Theory of the ancient theologians was wrong and the truth is that God manifests God's self in history in three modes: creator, savior, and continuing sustaining spirit. However, it is entirely the same God in each case, the entire divine being in every case, the same person in each case, the same Holy Spirit in each case; just different modes of appearance or manifestation and function. That is what I mean when I say that I believe in the Holy Spirit, and that is also why I so believe.

The Hebrew Bible promised that the coming messiah/redeemer would be called, Immanuel, God with us. That name was attached to Jesus in the first birth narrative in the gospels. However, that did not mean that God would only be with us so long as Jesus was here, but rather that God keeps showing up in history so consistently that we can always keep on saying, Immanuel. God is with us, and continues to be, as Holy Spirit.

Now, if you look at the creed in that way, it starts to take on a much fresher and more meaningful shape. It means that the creed is trying to say to us that we are confessing three things with the apostolic church of all ages. First, we are affirming what we know God is like as father and what God does in that role. "I believe in God the father almighty." That is what God is like. What God does as father is function as creator of the material universe, a thing that is empirically evident to us as obvious truth every time we open our eyes and look around.

Second, in reciting the Creed, we are affirming what we know God as Son or Brother is like, "I believe in Jesus Christ, God's unique Son, our Lord, who was conceived by God in a woman, and born of Mary." That is what God is like as Son of Mankind. What he does as Son of Man is function as the one "suffering under Pontius Pilate, crucified, dead, buried, risen, ascended, and enthroned in heaven in divine glory."

Third, in confessing our faith by means of the Apostles' Creed we declare that we know what God is like when God shows up in history and life *today*. God comes to us as the movement of an inner Spirit in our spirits. What God does as inner spirit is plain in the creed. God manifests himself as Spirit in our palpable experiences of the Holy Universal Church, that is, in the communion of saints, and the forgiveness of sins. That is what God does and how God shows up now, in our time: inciting to life and vitality the believing communities world wide, embracing and inspiring us with the communion of the saints, intimating to us our forgiveness: forgiveness in advance, forgiveness always, forgiveness for everything, forgiveness for evermore. I believe in the Holy Spirit because I experience those manifestations and intimations of God's utter and unconditional acceptance of me—of us all—in the here and now (see the extended discussion of forgiveness in chapter 17 below).

The church has always been afraid of the Holy Spirit. That is probably the result of two things, at least. The nature of the Holy Spirit, as promised by Christ, is ethereal and intangible. God, as spirit, functions through the intimations, inspirations, motivations, consolations, reassurances, illuminations, and affirmations of us as humans, as we are making our way in the tragic adventure of life. These consolations and intimations are sometimes mediated through tangible means, such as by some of the words of the scripture, or by a word of guidance from a mentor or a preacher or a friend. Therefore, the Spirit can never be predictable or controllable.

The Divine Spirit speaks to one person now and to another then, to some here and to others there, sometimes through one experience and at other times through another kind of experience. The Spirit speaks to us personally at times and at other times through a sense of being part of a community of faith. Jesus said, "The Spirit is like the wind. It blows where and when it will. Like the wind you cannot see where it is coming from or where it is going, but like the wind you can see the effect it has on us and on our world."

The Holy Spirit, and God's behavior or work as Holy Spirit, cannot be quantified, packaged, defined, or crafted into a theological proposition. That fact has always felt uncomfortable for the church - particularly for the church as organization and institution, where things need to be so tied down that we can capture them in a creed, a Book of Confessions, or a Book of Church Order. Consequently, the church has always been preoccupied with Jesus Christ, that is, with the church's Christology. Jesus is a tangible phenomenon of history that can be studied scientifically and packaged in theological propositions. These sound like eternal truth until you start to examine them. The truth about Jesus is, of course, of central importance; but even Tertullian (ca. 160–ca. 220 CE)—who defined many of the crucial terms of Christian theology in the early period of the church, thus setting forth the foundational concepts later used in the early creeds of the church—left the church when the bishops put the authority of the bishops before the creed, and the authority of the creed before the Bible, and the authority of the Bible before the personal intimations of the Holy Spirit in the hearts and spirits of individual Christians. He said the bishops were "ruling the Holy Spirit out of the church."

Therefore, it has always been more comfortable to the church to make an idolatry out of propositions about Jesus Christ as God, than live with the expectation of the Spirit getting loose in the church and leading us, through its unpredictable intimations, into the truth about God. What would it look like if God blew through all the different kinds of believing communities as Holy Spirit, like a metaphorical flaming fire and rushing windstorm, as at Pentecost? Would we put up with that? Would we know what to do with it? Would we recognize it as the presence and power of God for this day and age? Could it work to enliven and vitalize spirituality in all of us again in this 21st century? What if we prayed for the Spirit and let the Spirit of God loose in our lives, thoughts, and expectations? For me the reality and truth of this line in the creed is the most important part of the whole creed. It eclipses all the problem aspects in the creed that come before it.

Now, if you read the creed carefully, you will notice that what God as Holy Spirit has been busy trying to do in the world for the last twenty centuries is: 1) to vitalize a holy universal believing community; 2) to engender in all of us a unity of communion as God's saints; and 3) to get across to us the radical nature of his forgiveness of all humanity in advance of our being born. I think there is supposed to be a colon right after the words, "Holy Spirit," in the Creed. "I believe in the Holy Spirit: the holy universal church, the communion of saints, and the forgiveness of sins." Those are the experiential and empirical expressions of God as the Holy Spirit alive and well in the world—in our world in our day—today. I believe in God as Father: creator. I believe in God as Son: savior. I believe in God as Holy Spirit: church, relationship, forgiveness. Another graphic way of saying that last one is: *Holy Spirit-in-the-world is believing-community-as-community-of-forgiveness.*

In the darkest hour of my adult life, when I thought all was lost for me, the Holy Spirit spoke to me in an audible voice in the middle of the night and put in my head and heart Psalm 37:3a, "Trust in the Lord and do good!" After that I had no further anguish about the heresy trial I was enduring. The trouble that threatened to take away my livelihood and ministry went away by itself. I was condemned on five counts in 1974 and vindicated on a technicality in 1975, without lifting a finger regarding it to defend myself. It was all of the Holy Spirit.

At another period of great difficulty for me, God unexpectedly gave me another son who cheered my soul and filled my life with meaning and perpetual joy that shall last until I die—and I think, through all eternity.

During another time when I was suffering a siege of great doubt and spiritual mystification, I was awakened in the middle of the night by a forcible, repeated rap on the back of my hand. Someone was trying to get my attention. I opened one eye to see who it was. No one was there, but through the window right in front of my face was arrayed in magnificent display, the alignment of Venus, the moon, and Jupiter. My mind was immediately filled with a sense of the presence of the Holy Spirit, reminding me that God is closer than a brother all the time, as the Bible says. It was a natural phenomenon, of course, just the moon and two planets. That alignment happens every so often. But that is not the point. Someone who was there but invisible wrapped on my hand and awoke me, and then when I saw that phenomenon in the sky, right through my window, right in front of my face the way I lay in bed, quite involuntarily and spontaneously the experience filled me with a sense of the holy and the presence of God. I did not decide upon reflection that it meant that. My whole self was simply filled with that sense of things at a level that was vastly sub-cognitive and sub-volitional. It was just there, filling my whole self with a sense of infinitely consoling wonder.

God does not always show up as Holy Spirit in spectacular and para-psychological ways, to all of us or all the time, as he did to me in those three life-changing events, and at a number of other spectacular ones in my life. Most of the time, I experience the Spirit in the growth-inducing and meaning-filled ways in which life unfolds in the rational world of every day life; especially in the way in which the divine spirit has taken the times of suffering in my life and turned them into remarkable times of growth, insight, and illumination.

The story is told of Professor Benjamin Breckinridge Warfield, a famous theologian at Princeton Theological Seminary, being stopped one morning in the middle of a profound theological lecture on divine providence. A friend burst into his classroom and enjoined Warfield to stop everything and pray with him a prayer of thanksgiving for a supernatural providence. He declared that God had just saved him from a horrible fate. He was driving down Stockton Street when a dog scared his horses and the team ran away out of control. His buggy was smashed, one of the horses badly injured, and he was thrown clear and escaped with hardly a scratch.

Dr. Warfield agreed to stop everything to pray with him for this special divine providence and tangible intervention of the sustaining Divine Spirit, provided the man would then take the time to pray with Dr. Warfield for an equal or even greater manifestation of God's providential presence in Dr. Warfield's experience. The man agreed. They knelt and thanked God for sparing the man in his crisis. Then Dr. Warfield continued and thanked God for the fact that he had been driving his horses and buggy down Stockton Street for forty years, and nothing ever spooked his horses, and they never fled out of control, and Dr. Warfield also came through all those vulnerable years without a scratch.

God as Holy Spirit shows up usually in very ordinary ways, at very ordinary moments, in very ordinary experiences. The thing is to have the eyes to see and ears to hear how God shows up around the next corner! God always does and always will—as the divine presence—as Holy Spirit.

9

Resurrection of the Body

St. Paul emphatically hung all of Christian hope upon the resurrection. The most important chapter in the Bible in which he explains this is 1 Corinthians 15. There he is quite assertive in claiming that the resurrection of all humans is certified by the fact and truth of Jesus' resurrection. Therefore, chapters 6 and 9 in this book are inevitably tied closely together. In verse 9 of his resurrection chapter, Paul declares that if there is no resurrection, then Christ has not been resurrected. Moreover, if Christ has not been raised from the dead, then our faith is futile and our salvation is null and void. He concludes these ruminations with striking words. "If in this life we who are in Christ have *only hope*, we are to be greatly pitied" (RSV).

It is clear that Paul means to say that we certainly know Christ was raised from the dead, so in this life we not only have *hope* but we have *certainty* about our own resurrection and eternal life after this life. However, there is an enigma here for Paul, and so also for us who read Paul. It lies in what he calls the mystery of the resurrection. His entire argument throughout I Corinthians 15 is about this mystery, indeed, it is a two sided mystery. It is the mystery about the nature of Jesus' resurrection and the mystery about the nature of our own resurrections. It has to do with what resurrection really means or entails.

After making a long story of persuading us about the truth of Jesus' resurrection and its importance for us, Paul wraps up that part of the chapter with the amazing observation that Jesus *died in the flesh but he rose in the spirit* (1 Cor 15:44). To our great surprise, Peter says exactly this same thing (1 Pet 3:18), as I pointed out in chapter 6, above, when I was responding to that line in the Creed that says "The third day he rose again from the dead."

The mystery for Paul, apparently, lay in the fact that he had heard from the disciples the reports of Jesus' appearances. Perhaps his own encounter with the resurrected Jesus on the Damascus road, leading to personal conversion, was of a similar experience as the resurrection appearances reported by the disciples. The narratives of Jesus appearances after the resurrection made him realize that the body Jesus had after the resurrection was a different body than he had before the resurrection. Before the resurrection, Jesus' body was a physical and material body, and afterward his body was a spiritual and nonmaterial body. That is why he could enter rooms by just manifesting there, eat if he wished but not need to eat, move long distances without time delay, and be recognized by others, but only after he chose to reveal himself to them in some characteristic way. Paul refers to this spiritual body of Jesus as his glorified body, and declares that we are also going to have that kind of glorified body in our life after this life.

That is why Paul spends the last half of this resurrection chapter carefully setting forth for us that there are material bodies that are of this earth, physical; and there are spiritual bodies that are of a heavenly nature. These are remarkably different, according to Paul. So the resurrection involves being raised to a new kind of glorified body. It does not involve the resurrection of the old physical body that was buried. Paul emphasizes the differences between these two kinds of bodies so repeatedly (1 Cor 15:35–55) that it is clear how much of a mystery this is for him and how tough he thinks it is to get it across to us clearly and memorably.

He might very well have so much concern, because for 2,000 years the believing community of the Christian churches has refused to accept what he was saying so carefully and repeatedly. Christian believers have continued throughout history to claim that we must believe in a literal resurrection of this material body that is laid in the grave. Think of the many discussions Christians have had about how God will gather together all the atoms and molecules of all our bodies on the last day of history and put us all back together again in the resurrection.

Think of the debates throughout history about whether it was appropriate for a Christian to be cremated instead of buried. Christians once thought the body should be preserved to the extent possible, against the day of resurrection. That sounds something like pagan Egyptian death-theology. Today, of course, many think that whether we are oxidized by

Resurrection of the Body

fire or by decay makes little difference. However, even many of those Christians, who think it makes little difference, take that position with the assumption and trust that God can figure out how to put everyone back together again when the time comes.

Then there were also those strange discussions about where God would find room in heaven for all the people who will be resurrected, from all the years of the long reach of time. I have often chuckled about the fact that such a question seemed like a real issue to some folks. However, before we set aside all those kinds of notions, let us look again carefully at the creed. The line before us just now is, "I believe in the resurrection of the body." Obviously, the authors of the creeds were greatly concerned about these very issues. They wanted to make sure that it was clearly nailed down in the Apostles' Creed and in some of the other Ecumenical Creeds that the only proper way to interpret the New Testament was to insist upon the literal resurrection of the material body that was physically planted in the ground.

If those bishops, who represented all the sections of the Christian church throughout the Mediterranean world, had wished to *represent St. Paul* more honestly, they could simply have written a line in the creed that affirmed the resurrection and allowed us to read Paul in an unprejudiced way. Or they might have read Paul correctly and written instead, "I believe in resurrection to a glorified body," or "to a spiritual state." Paul makes it plain that what he is talking about is the fact that the person must put off materiality and put on spirituality, put off mortality and put on immortality, put off perishability and put on imperishability, put off the physical and put on the ethereal, put off the fleshly and put on the heavenly, that is, the spiritual. He declares this fourteen times, in various metaphors, in that one resurrection chapter (1 Corinthians 15).

Yet the bishops who wrote the creed went to great pains to insist upon a *bodily* resurrection. They made certain that the Apostles' Creed said specifically, "I believe in the resurrection of the body." Moreover, most Christians have tended to follow this official doctrine ever since, to the great mystification of some of us. Undoubtedly, this is in part due to the fact that the Athanasian Creed, written in the same era as the Apostles' Creed, and basically by the same bishops, is even more assertive on this point. It moves to its close with these words, "He [Jesus] ascended into heaven. He sits on the right hand of the Father, God Almighty. From thence he shall come to judge the living and the dead; at whose coming all men *shall rise again with their bodies*; and shall give account of their own works ... This is the catholic [universal Christian] faith, which except a man believe faithfully, he cannot be saved." What bunk that is!

It is the clear teaching of the New Testament that each of us will enjoy a blessed resurrection and that the outcome of it will be spiritual. We will be given a new spiritual body, like Christ's glorified body. It will not be limited by time, space, or materiality. We will recognize each other as having familiar characteristics but we will connect only when we wish to reveal ourselves to each other. Everyone will be filled with grace and graciousness; and love will reign supreme in that transcendent world.

Moreover, it is implied in this Pauline teaching on the resurrection, and confirmed by the gospel of John, that we do not need to wait in some state of sleep or limbo until a final date at the end of history when we will hear the trumpet sound and be raised from the dead. All the speculation or dogma about those kinds of things is foolishness. Jesus and Paul both made it clear that death means for all of us that we go immediately to be with the Lord our God, the Blessed Father of us all. The trumpet call for each of us is that moment of transition from time to eternity. That is when every eye shall see him, every knee bow, and every tongue confess that Christ is Lord, to the glory of God the Father.

John's gospel is the one written after the church had many decades to reflect upon the meaning of Christ's life, message, resurrection, and intention for the world. According to that gospel there will be no cataclysmic end to history, no second coming, and no final judgment day for all of humanity. John and Paul agree that the judgment day for each of us is the moment we die. Then we shall go to be with the Lord and see him face to face. We will all cry out as did Thomas at Jesus' appearance, "My Lord and my God!" The judgment that will be pronounced upon each of us will be the declaration of God's grace, "Enter into the joy of your Lord," "For by grace we are saved through faith, and that not of ourselves, it is a gift of God, not of works, lest any one of us should boast that we are worthy" (Eph 2:8–9).

So, I believe in the resurrection of the dead and I expect the fullness of eternal life. I must honestly say that I think those bishops who wrote the Nicene Creed were trying harder to tell the truth Paul was at such pains to get across to us, than the bishops who wrote the Apostles' Creed. I like their formulation of this line in the Nicene Creed much better than in the Apostles' Creed or the Athanasian Creed. The Nicene Creed concludes, "I believe in the one holy catholic and apostolic church ... and I look for the resurrection of the dead, and the life of the world to come." I say, "Amen!" to that. So be it, by God's grace!

10

Life Everlasting

WE HAVE COME TO the last proposition of the Apostles Creed. "I believe in the life *everlasting*." Clearly the saints of the Hebrew Bible hoped against hope that God would afford them a joyful and vibrant life with God after death and Sheol. The New Testament developed that theme elaborately. Both the gospels and the Pauline epistles hold out the hope of *eternal* life with God. The Book of the Revelation of St. John creates a wildly fanciful and symbolic scenario about the ultimate transcendental destiny of all things. Most of us automatically coalesce Paul's extensive teaching about *eternal* life with this idea of *everlasting* life as it appears in the creed. The two concepts are related; but they are, nonetheless, quite different. Reflecting on their difference and their connection can illumine our vision of faith.

The Pauline notion of *eternal* life is about *quality* of life and the creed's claim for *everlasting* life is about *quantity*. Paul's idea of *eternal* life is a remarkably innovative one in which he conceives of the possibility of our participating in the quality of God's kind of life now. We do this in our earthly life as we pursue the quest of faith and as we hope in God's grace and goodness to us. Paul imagines that the experience of the believer is of such a sort that we can enjoy life with God, as it were, in the here and now. He describes his own experience of Christian faith in God's grace as the process of such a different kind of existence that he realizes in a tangible way, in his mundane life now, the relief, joy, security, consolation, and sense of blessedness that is surely the nature of the heavenly existence with God after death.

When we read Romans 8 and 1 Corinthians 13 and 15, as well as numerous other choice passages from the Pauline literature, we have a clear sense as to why Paul understands eternal life as he does. He frequently describes this earthly life as an ordeal in which we are rather constantly living with perplexities about our morality and our mortality, filled with fear, guilt, and shame, consistently falling short of the mark of God's ideal for us and our own best hopes and intentions for ourselves. Paul calls this experience a "constant dying" or a "constant struggle with the deadliness within us." In this context of mortal struggle, Paul came to a dramatic sense of faith and trust in God. He saw in Jesus good reasons to believe that God is not a God of threat, before whose face our mundane ordeal is a grave danger for us; a god whose primary objective is judgment of evildoers. He knew God is not in the business of shaping us up but of cheering us up.

Paul realized that the entire point of Jesus' ministry was to get across the insight that John's gospel later clarifies so crisply. That truth is that God is a God of unconditional, radical, and universal grace, forgiveness, and acceptance of us all, as we are. Grace is radical in the sense that God totally accepts us just as we are and not as we should or will be. Grace cuts through and outflanks all our legalistic and defensive desires for self-justification and declares that we do not need to justify ourselves because God already has justified us. Grace is universal in the sense that no human being, nor any aspect of creation, shall be unredeemed—no sinner or saint left behind. Grace is unconditional because it is an unearned gift to every human being, in spite of ourselves.

Paul's life was changed by the realization that by that kind of grace we are saved, and that not of ourselves but as a *gift* of God, not of our efforts, lest any of us should be able to boast that we did it on our own, that we justified ourselves. He describes, in numerous places in his epistles, this amazing new sense of relief, joy, security, and blessedness, but especially in the letter to the church in Ephesus (2:8–9) and in Romans 8. He is sure that this sense of the eternal quality of life in the spirit of a believer, here and now, puts us already upon the plain on which God lives and is alive and vital to us. It is the quality of life one has in living with God in God's kind of world, now and forever, with God's kind of spirit. That is what Paul calls eternal life: now and forever.

It is remarkable, it seems to me, that the authors of the creed did not fix solidly upon this Pauline concept and enshrine it in our Confession of Faith, as the final affirmation of the creed. That Pauline way of looking at things seems to me much more important for us to celebrate than the idea that some state of after life is going to go on forever, *everlastingly*. Surely the bishops of the church, in that ancient moment in time, knew the Pauline notion very well. Furthermore, they had just finished making sure that the nature and work of God as Holy Spirit in the world was carefully explained in the creed. That must have made them think of Paul. They must have recalled his dramatic conversion on the Road to Damascus and related that in their minds to what they had just said about the Holy Spirit. They must have relished, as we do today, the only hope for any human, which is described so well in the Pauline biblical literature. Surely they had caught that central, redemptive, life-changing insight that Paul sets forth as the human conversion to life on God's eternal plain of heaven-like relief, joy, security, blessedness, and consolation; when we know that God has removed all fear, guilt, and shame from the equation of our relationship with him.

So why did they not say, "I believe in the life eternal," a much more profound concept than the claim of the creed, "I believe in the life everlasting"? I honestly think that it is difficult to discern the answer to my question. Were they reacting to some philosophy afloat in their day that suggested life ends at death, and so they wanted to nail down their faith that life goes on after death? That might prompt them to focus on making the point about "life everlasting," a matter of quantity rather than Paul's sense of quality. Or did they have some other kind of perspective in mind which made a celebration of the unending character of life after death more important than Paul's notion that the life of faith starts the heavenly experience now, and continues when we "go to be with the Lord" at death, thus making death merely a step across another threshold of personal development?

Perhaps the real story is this. They assumed that the Pauline idea was so central a part of the experience of the believer, and so universally held by the community everywhere, that the thing for them to do in the creed was to emphasize again that this redemptive quality of life and experience simply goes on forever and ever, beyond all possible human imagination, timelessly. They may have meant to close the creed and leave us with the sensation that we always have when we try to envision infinity. Where does it begin and end? When you set your camera lens on infinity, how far can you see? When you reflect upon the mathematical equation that includes the symbol and concept of infinity, what does it say to you? Nobody knows!

It is relatively easy to comprehend what *quality* of life Paul is referring to when he speaks of *eternal* life, since we can experience that level of life in communion with God here and now. It is life lived in the peace and relief of the certainty of God's forgiving grace. However, nobody knows just what the *quantity* of *everlasting* life is, or can possibly mean. Only God knows, and he takes care of it. To say, "I believe in the life everlasting" is to say, "I do not know what I am talking about, so I throw myself into God's arms. I trust God for that incomprehensibility." I am sure God knows what the *infinity* factor in the *eternal* equation stands for, and that is enough for me.

PART TWO

How the Divine Spirit Really Works in Our Daily Lives

11

Honest to God

HAVING WRITTEN ALL THIS about our faith traditions and the presence of the Holy Spirit, it is now important to ask how we are to carry ourselves operationally. How is God in history and how shall we carry ourselves in a way that is pragmatically honest to God? How do faith claims give us a sense of the truth by which to live? I firmly believe that most humans really want to understand things accurately and do things right. Earnest humans have great differences and disagreements about what we understand accurately and what we think it is right to do. These disparities arise mostly out of our dependence upon vastly different life experiences. We each have widely differing information about what is the truth and the right, and surprisingly different perceptions of the meaning of it all.

When I was a senior officer of the active U.S. Army, with numerous subordinates responsible to me and senior officers to whom I was accountable, I remember often hearing and saying, "There is your way of doing this, and there is my way of doing this, and there is the Army way of doing it. Forget about the many options. Do it the Army way." In most cases it is true that any given course of action may be carried out in a variety of ways. Most of us conclude from that fact that the right thing is usually not one thing but a great variety of possible right things.

Similarly, most people today, I find, believe that truth is not one clear and definable fact or one identifiable way of understanding a thing, situation, or idea. Most people think that truth is a variety of possible ways of looking at any given matter. Aristotle thought that there is a great difference between objective truth and popular opinion. He said in his book on ethics, "The high minded person must care more for the truth, than for what people think"¹ It would be hard to disagree with Aristotle.

My wife is *absolutely* sure that truth is not absolute or objective. She is certain that there is such a thing as her truth, which is always remarkably different from my truth. I keep telling her that what she calls her truth is really only her perception and that truth stands on its own two feet, out there in the wind and the rain, quite apart from what we may think it is, and that it is our job to try to make certain that our perceptions are as close to that objective truth as possible. When I say that to her, I am always secretly aware of the fact that I think my truth is closer to the Truth than hers is. Truth stands on its own merit, outside of our minds and even outside of God's mind, if we are to take seriously Proverbs 8–9 and Job 28. In those chapters, truth (personified, as Wisdom) engages in the task of tutoring God on how to create the universe.

Harry Emerson Fosdick, the world-famous preacher at the Riverside Church in New York for many decades, declared regarding the objectivity of truth and of our quest for it, "One of the *supreme moments of human experience* arrives when a man [or woman] gets his [or her] eye on something concerning which he [or she] is persuaded that it is the eternal truth."²

Well, fifty-five years of such rather vigorous conversation between Mary Jo and me has not made a dint in her concept of truth, but I can secretly confess to you here that her line of argument has made a dint in my concept of the truth. Indeed, it has illumined it considerably. I have come to realize that each of us is only able to possess the truth to the extent that we can gather knowledge about it, understand that data, and integrate it into our way of thinking about things, human and divine. That is, the scope of the truth that each of us possesses at any given time is the truth upon which we are called by God and by our own integrity to operate. So that is *the truth* for us at this moment, our personal truth, as Mary Jo insists.

---

1. Aristotle (240 BCE), *Nicomachean Ethics*, in W. E. Ross, trans., revised by J. O Urmson, in Jonathan Barnes, ed. (1984), *The Complete Works of Aristotle, The Revised Oxford Translation*, Vol. 2, Bollingen Series 51/2 (Princeton: Princeton University Press, 1729–1867).

2. Fosdick, *A Great Time to Be Alive: Sermons on Christianity in Wartime* (New York: Harper & Brothers, 1944). See also Fosdick, *A Guide to Understanding the Bible: The Development of Ideas within the Old and New Testament* (New York: Harper & Brothers, 1938).

She has good authority to back her claim. A thoughtful American philosopher named Bede Jarrett declared in 1915, in his book *Meditations for Living Fully*, "The Truth may be one, final, and determined; but my apprehension of it can never be anything of the kind; it is changing continuously."[3] He was very much in line with St. Augustine's notion 1550 years earlier, "Turn not to the outside world! Into your own self go back! In the inner person resides Truth!"[4]

I take it, therefore, that when Jesus declared that if we know the truth, the truth will set us free, he was looking at the issue of the truth from both sides. On the one hand, it is clear from the context that he was encouraging us to quest for an understanding of the truth as God sees it. That truth comes from the mind of God and holds its own, as truth, regardless of what our opinions or perceptions of it might be, and regardless what the bishops wrote in the Apostle's Creed, or what we think of what they wrote. In fact, the specific truth of which Jesus was speaking in John 8:32 was the truth that he was the Son of Man. That meant that Jesus was the messenger from heaven who came to reveal the mysteries of God to us. Those mysteries, according to Paul, are epitomized in the fact that, "God was in Christ reconciling the world unto himself."

On the other hand, it is clear that when Jesus said this truth would make us free, he was speaking of something happening inside of us in so far as we comprehend these truths of God. That is, Jesus was urging us to be authentic persons of inner integrity about the truth, in so far as we understand it. We must hold that much of the truth as we understand, as though it is God's *whole truth* for us, and be absolutely open and honest with ourselves about believing, speaking, and living in keeping with *that truth* that we perceive. Honest to ourselves and therefore, honest to God!

In 1963 Bishop J. A. T. Robinson wrote *Honest to God*, a book in which he argued that since we can only speak of God in metaphors, we must make sure that we are not slavishly devoting ourselves to the metaphors and language of past Christian tradition, just because it is the tradition of our doctrine, theology, church dogma, or the Apostles' Creed.[5]

---

3. Bede Jarrett, *Meditations for Living Fully* (1915; reprinted, New York: Sophia Institute Press, 2005).

4. Aurelius Augustine (390 CE), *On True Religion*, in Whitney J. Oates, ed., *Basic Writings of Saint Augustine*, vol. 1 (New York: Random House, 1948).

5. John A. T. Robinson, *Honest to God* (Philadelphia: Westminster, 1963). See also Robinson, *The Human Face of God* (Philadelphia: Westminster, 1973); Robinson,

Language flavors and meanings change over time and so we cannot be sure that what we mean by our creeds and traditions today is what the authors of the creeds or of our theology really understood by them back then. We cannot reenter their moment and its atmosphere, to perceive again what meaning freight of thought and feeling their words carried precisely for them. We may read with great profit the grand words of St. Thomas Aquinas (13th century), for example, and greatly admire his wonderfully surprising framework of thought, fashioned like a cathedral of ideas; but we cannot reenter his mind and spirit and be sure we are discerning the precise thought and feeling he was conceiving and trying to convey.

We must ask ourselves what the truth of our faith means for us operationally. The God described by the past is dead. The God of the gaps in our knowledge cannot be alive to us. The God of threat and of magical religion is not vitally alive in our day. God must come alive for us in our faith experience in the present, in terms of *our best understanding* of the historic testimony of our faith traditions and the rubrics of life's meaning now. This acquisition of the truth for our own way of understanding God, ourselves, and our world can only come by the illumination and leading of the Holy Spirit, as we try to understand the historic faith. To make this happen we must be open to and trust the intimations of the spirit of God to our spirits personally, daily.

We might say that we must take the position and posture that Peter took at the Sea of Galilee when Jesus asked him three times if Jesus could count on his love. Peter realized Jesus was pressing him three times, just as he had betrayed Jesus three times when Jesus was on trial in Caiaphas' garden. Jesus asked him, "Can I count on you being willing to invest your life in the truth you have learned about me?" Peter responded in effect, "Lord, you know me better than I know myself. You heard me betray you. Obviously, I am a limited and flawed human being with a limited and flawed comprehension of the truth about myself, to say nothing about the mysteries regarding you and God. You must take me as I am. I am a mere man who must operate with only that truth that I have acquired and that I can learn from careful thought and from the school of hard

---

In the End God (New York: Harper & Row, 1968); Robinson, *Explorations into God*, (London: SCM, 1967); and David L. Edwards, *The Honest to God Debate* (Philadelphia: Westminster, 1963).

knocks in life. But I am *for* what you are *for* in so far as I can understand it." Jesus ordained him on the spot!

I mentioned my Princeton professor, Otto Piper, earlier in these pages. I once asked him how we can be sure that what we understand is really God's truth. You remember that his response was astonishing to me at the time. He said, "Well, when you notice that your own personal spiritual experience rings true to the witness of the scripture and to the testimony of the historic church concerning its faith experience, you are probably on fairly solid ground." That is the key. That key to the world is given into our hands, when we throw ourselves unreservedly into the service of the highest truth we know. You might be surprised by my quoting in this context from the Qur'an, to the following point, "The truth is from your Lord. Let him who will, believe it! Let him who will, reject it!"[6] Throwing oneself into the service of the highest truth we can comprehend affords us faith that enhances life and character. Every one of us can testify to the fact that it works that way. Fundamentalisms, that is, obsessive preoccupation with ideologies for their own sake, apart from real inner experience of the healing and freeing power of God's truth, always wreck life and character.

So we are simply not permitted, if we pursue the truth, to confuse truth with creed, tradition, theology, dogma, ideology, doctrine, revelation, or even the Bible. It may be the case that they express truth, if properly understood; but they tell the truth, not because they are doctrine or ideology or revelation. All those artifacts of the faith tell the truth when they cause something to happen inside of us: an awakening, as an individual or as the community of believers that makes our inner experience of God and his world fill our lives with consolation, peace, assurance, and hope. From this arises the quality of wholesome life and thought that comes from trust in God's grace. That experience is properly called faith in the truth of God, even though it is actually only our comprehension of it—our personal truth.

There are many ways to know the truth about God, and about ourselves and our world. We can know such truth by experience, by rational thought, by ESP, prescience, intuition, and by the testimony of others. Cardinal Newman thought that there is no ultimate test of truth besides the testimony borne to truth by the mind and spirit of each of us as we

---

6. Qur'an, surah 18:29.

sense its authenticity.[7] That sounds like a very subjective approach to our quest for God's truth and subjectivism can be narcissistic, self-centered, and dangerous.

Karl Barth was one of the greatest Protestant theologians of the twentieth century. He was so afraid of the subjectivism he found in the work of Friedrich Schleiermacher, probably the greatest theologian of the nineteenth century, that Barth completely condemned Schleiermacher's work. He thought Schleiermacher's theology was subjectivistic because he emphasized so strongly the individual Christian's perception of the intimations of the divine spirit. Schleiermacher admittedly personalized the realization of God's presence to us and in our life experience. Barth effectively suppressed the influence of this very important theologian and pastor for a century. In the end Barth had to apologize and reckon with the fact that Schleiermacher's highly personalized sense of spirituality, and of the ministry of the spirit of God to our spirits, was probably one of the most spiritually insightful perspectives since Jesus himself.

That emphasis upon God speaking by his spirit directly to the spirit of each individual person is dangerous, of course. People like Adolf Hitler and the Muslim terrorists really believe that they know and are obeying the truth God has given to them when they kill innocent people for their cause. It is plain to see that their perception is evil. They do not get their truth from the spirit of God or from the spirit of the good and healing nature of godliness. That is why the Bible requires us to discern the spirits to see if they be of God, that is, to discern whether they enhance our lives, characters, and healing relationships, or degrade them. If the truth operates redemptively, it certifies itself. It is of the Spirit. Its results are wholesome and healing. If the results are destructive, it is not of the Spirit. The Bible implies that we can figure out the difference if we consistently try for truth and its fruitfulness: a wholesome life of love and grace.

At best in life, we have limited data, but we must invest our time in diligent learning to do the best we can with what we have. We need not worry that our sense of the truth, even about God and the faith, is narrowed to our private outlook and limited capacity to grasp God's truth. Jesus assures us that our own limited truth will set us free because he knows that to be true to ourselves is a way of being honest to God. That is completely freeing. It frees us from fear, guilt, shame, ignorance, con-

---

7. John Henry Cardinal Newman, *An Essay in Aid of a Grammar of Assent*, with an Introduction by Etienne Gilson, (Garden City, NY: Doubleday Image Books, 1955).

fusion, and perplexity. It affords us that sense of freedom which brings spiritual consolation, peace, and tranquility. It gives us a life of trust and assurance, and clear-headed, clear-hearted confidence.

When that sense of open, honest, freedom is illumined by a sense of God's unconditional grace for us, we are free indeed. We can *trust our own insights, our own spiritual quest, our own sense of honest inner congruency*. We can *trust our personal truth quest*. Even a mustard seed's worth of true faith in God's grace is saving faith. The OT prophet encouraged us to trust that God meant it when he said, "If with all your heart you truly seek me, you shall ever surely find me!" That must be what Jesus wanted us to hear in his words, "God's spirit will lead you into all the truth" (John 14:26).

So if the traditions, creeds, historic theology, or even the Bible, just do not make sense to you, do not believe it or claim that you do. Be honest to God and yourself. *Honest* error is better than *dishonest* reasons for mouthing or holding to any notion. In his best chapter in the New Testament (1 Corinthians 13) Paul declared that at best we now see reality as puzzling reflections in a mirror ("through a glass, darkly," KJV). We look for that day when we shall see the truth whole and face to face. On that day "we shall know reality as thoroughly as God now knows us" (J. B. Philips).

If some teaching does not yet ring true for you, wait on the spirit. Seek the leading of the spirit. *Throw yourself unreservedly into the service of the highest truth you know*. Go courageously with it, while listening carefully to the outlook of others on the matter. Open yourself to the spirit. If you adhere to a formulation of the truth just because it is our faith tradition, you have substituted ideology for truth. That is idolatry. Then you are neither honest to God, nor to yourself. Reinhold Niebuhr declared, "It is neither possible for man [or woman] to know the truth fully, nor to avoid the error of pretending that he [or she] does."[8]

Let us not pretend. Let us wait on the Lord to lead and illumine us, daily, existentially. It is intriguing to live life with an eye open to how the Divine Spirit will show up around the next corner. Let us be Christians who are open to the light and truth from that Spirit. If with all our hearts we truly seek God, we shall ever surely find God. We shall know God's truth and that truth will set us free! The Bible says that if the truth has set us free, the truth of our perception, we are really free.

---

8. Reinhold Niebuhr, *Human Destiny*, in *The Nature and Destiny of Man*, 1 vol. edition (New York: Charles Scribner, 1943).

12

Why I Believe in God

I BELIEVE IN GOD because of lilies. Well, maybe I should say irises, since I think they are the most beautiful flower in God's world. Jesus once said, "Consider the lilies of the field how they grow. They toil not, neither do they spin, yet Solomon in all his glory was not arrayed like one of these." If he had lived in North American, I am sure he would have liked irises better even than lilies. If he would not, he should have, of course!

It seems to me that everything we have worked through so far in this volume requires me to reveal why I look for God's spirit to show up around each corner of life. Why do I believe in God? Moreover, this is a good time in my life and work to address it. When I was a young seminary student, preaching one of my first sermons, I selected the passage from the Lord's Prayer that says "Forgive us our debts as we forgive our debtors." My intention was to develop an elaborated theology of forgiveness. I preached vigorously, valiantly, articulately, and long. When I was departing the sanctuary, an elderly lady took my hand and said to me sweetly, "Young man, you have not lived long enough to have sinned well enough to have been forgiven thoroughly enough to know what you are talking about."

One has to earn the right to speak on how God is to be discerned in history. Perhaps now, after nearly sixty years of ministry and seventy eight years of life, I have earned the right to speak on why I believe in God. It has everything to do with that text, "Consider the lilies." It is not an easy task. God is uncommonly subtle. He does not make himself boldly known to us. We can know God, and have a foundation for believing in God, only if after years of seasoning we have developed the eyes to see and the ears to hear the spirit of God in our life experiences.

As I outlined in chapter 1, there are, in my judgment, only five reasons why a person ought to believe in God. I would like to explain

Why I Believe in God

each of those reasons more extensively now, in this chapter on Why I Believe in God. None of the five reasons that seem so persuasive to me have to do primarily with Jesus Christ. The first one is the *mindfulness of creation*. I have been struck profoundly, during all the long years of my education, reading, thought, and reflection, by the amazing fact of the orderliness and design of this marvelous, created world. The deeper one looks into the majesty of the creation the more profound the intricacies and order of it seem to be.

Of course, for a century and a half, and in some ways much longer than that, the prevailing opinion in the world of science has been that all this came about somehow by accident. The truth is that this wonderful world in which we live and of which we are a majestic part, reflects the design of an ingenious and creative mind. I consider the notion that this world came about by accident to be the most laughable of all hypotheses. I have tried to think, for example, what it would be like if I had no personal sense of God; no particular tradition or driving motivation to seek out God. If I were simply interested in a very secular understanding of the nature and structure of the material world, I am certain that I would be compelled, in the end, to invent a notion of some kind of grand creator behind this grand creation. Sheer honesty would require it. I cannot imagine honestly trying to account for this mindful creation without seeing behind it an intentionally creative mind.

Some years ago numerous scientists touted the idea that the further you look into creation the more you discover chaos and entropy. It is called "chaos theory." I predicted thirty-five years ago that behind what then seemed to us to be chaos would soon surface a new level of integrated order. Scientists, in the 1940s through the 1960s, had crossed over a new boundary of insight, experience, and data in physics and astrophysics. We had not, however, developed a good model for organizing that new data. So things looked chaotic. That sense of chaos has now raised itself to a new level of order. We have discovered the scientific models that account for that larger, deeper view of reality in God's creation.

A book I recently read, written actually in 1917 by Eric Schrödinger, is worth reading again. It is titled, *What is Life?*[1] Schrödinger predicted that every scientific breakthrough would look like chaos until we devel-

---

1. Eric Schrödinger (1917), *What is Life, the Physical Aspects of the Living Cell* (Cambridge: Cambridge University Press, 1917; reprinted London: Folio Society, 2000).

oped the models to see the new order in the data. It is clear to me that the more I have studied this material world the more profoundly aware I am of the mindful God behind this cleverly created universe.

However, it is not just the mindful order in creation that compels me to believe. Of course, if that were all I had I would already have a lot of evidence that would draw me to God. But I might set that on the shelf and say, "Well that is one theory, one hypothesis. When I really get to know everything about everything I will probably have a completely different perspective." The truth is that this compelling evidence of the mindfulness of creation is reinforced in my soul by a careful look at the *benevolence of God's providence* in life and in history. "Consider the lilies of the field," Jesus said. Consider them! Not just with regard to the majestic mindfulness of creation evident in their beauty, and the wonderful orderliness by which they repeat, generation after generation, their surprising genetic reproduction. Consider the benevolence of providence that sustains and orders their processes and our unfolding lives throughout the long pull of history.

When I look back on my life of nearly eighty years, I can tell you honestly that those things in my life which I thought were the very important issues, that I would have pushed and shoved into place with might and mien, if I could have, turned out to be virtually irrelevant to the course and meaning of my life.

On the other hand, those things that I thought were the tragic moments, which God, if he had any brains in his head at all, would have prevented from happening to me, have become the hinges of my destiny. It is not an accident for that kind of insight to come out of the complexities and dangers of my life. God's providence has been a careful, mindful, growth-oriented shepherding of my life and history all the while.

Some folks look at history and focus on the tragic moments. They can only see the tragedy in those tragic moments and never can get beyond that with the eyes to see and the ears to hear the deeper meaning of it. They inevitably miss what the outcome and the fruitfulness of our pain and travail is. For those with eyes to see and ears to hear it is not difficult in retrospect to see the careful, kindly shepherding of God's benevolent providence in our lives.

During the Revolutionary War, when the Continental Congress was trying to hammer out a constitution for this budding United States and the Continental army under George Washington was in a bad way, a

Virginia statesman named John Paige wrote a letter to Thomas Jefferson. In it he quoted from the prophet Zachariah, "Thomas, we know that the race is not to the swift, nor the battle to the strong, and do you not think that an angel rides in this whirlwind and directs the storm?" Thomas Jefferson responded with a profound affirmation of that same faith, acknowledging the undergirding guidance of God's providence that made possible the surprising outcome of the founding moments of our nation.

The third reason I believe in God is the inescapable evidence of the *aesthetic urge* in everything in God's universe. Given half a chance, unobstructed by human intervention, everything in God's world seems to me always to be moving toward beauty. For whose eyes is the edelweiss that blossoms in a snowy crevice at 14,000 feet on Mount Everest? Who delights in that? Who celebrates the color, the texture, the delicacy, the beauty? Is beauty in this world created only for our eyes and our ears? Who sees that exquisite explosion of the most delicate kind of art in billions of sun sets everyday on all the uncountable planets in the whole universe? Who sees that and sings poetry because of it? For God's eyes! Not for God's eyes only, but at least first of all for God's eyes. That is why Jesus said, "Consider the lilies, Solomon in all his glory had nothing on them. He was not arrayed like one of those!"

Last spring as I got onto the expressway I suddenly saw something I had never noticed before. There in the abandoned terrain of the newly constructed entrance ramp into the expressway, land just sort of lost between the entrance and the highway, there suddenly had sprung up an incredible array of wildflowers. I would imagine there were probably a hundred varieties of the most magnificent blooms. Leave things alone for a little while and they burst into beauty. Why not ugliness, why not bareness? Why is everything in this world so irrepressibly vital, so full of life? Why is life so full of beauty? It moves from a dry, dead looking, ugly root, to a colorful growing plant, and on to magnificent blossom, and finally to its rich fruiting. Irrepressible aesthetics everywhere! Is this accident or is there some grand soul that sits above this cosmic circle and celebrates? Celebrates the flowers in the abandoned land in Farmington Hills! I like a God like that. How could I not believe in a God like that?

The fourth reason that I believe in God is the *healing kindness of God's unconditional acceptance of us*. Say that it is only a notion that sprung up in some human head. Say there is no divine magic behind that revelation. Say it is simply an idea we came into out of our pain; the notion that God is a God who is not a threat, as people used to think, but a God who reaches out to us in kindness. Carl Rogers said the only thing that works in human relationship is unconditional positive regard. Is that just a human idea?

Of course it is not just a human idea! The capacity of the human mind to imagine the notion of grace is an astonishing miracle of imagination. The capacity of the human soul to be able to comprehend, in all of the woundedness and tragedy of our humanness, the notion of unconditional forgiveness, is superhuman. *Grace is a divine thing.*

It is not possible for me to imagine this, unless there is a transcendental analogue of forgiveness, God's forgiving nature, which teases out of my heart and mind the sense that I have been embraced in love in spite of myself. Our gracious forgiving God is the heavenly analogue to which my longing for forgiveness and reconciliation to God is the analogy. That notion of grace is tailored to my hearts' main hurt. It is in me the analogy of that heavenly analogue. It reaches around all of my defenses, all of my fear and guilt and shame. That forgiving grace touches me at the center of my main problem of quandary, confusion, and sense of inadequacy and shame. It neutralizes all the fear and guilt I may project into my relationship with myself and with God. It takes them away. Grace erases fear, guilt, and shame from the equation of my relationship with God.

That notion of grace makes it possible for me to accept my past with humble relief and consolation and leave it with God. He cancels its dangerousness with forgiveness. God frees me to make my present moments productive, so that I have a fruitful future. God is like a huge dynamo who creates all around him a huge force field of grace. We are like small electric motors. When God's force field of grace, i.e., his divine spirit, moves close to us so we are caught into the divine force field, our motor of spirituality turns on and hums away with the relief, freedom, security, assurance, and divine affirmation that heals us.

Grace makes it possible for me to accept the present with joyful responsibility despite my human limitations, and to do so with a sense of humor. Grace makes it possible for me to accept my future with confidence and hope so it may be a useable future in spite of whatever the anguish of my past. I believe in God because *grace is so relevant to my central need that if it had not been revealed in scripture I would have had to invent it to survive.* It is an ingenious divine arrangement that gives rich meaning to human lives, regardless of how damaged and distorted. God is the source and guarantor of my experience that love works and grace heals.

That leads me to the fifth reason to believe in God. It seems to me that when I take the perspective I have developed here, and I look at my own history, there seems to be in the middle of it all the subtle evidence that what is really going on here is that God is constantly insinuating himself into my experience. I can say that the whole of history is the enterprise of incarnation. It is like God clothing himself as it were in the flesh of human lives and subtly revealing himself in our sense of things and our sense of the presence of the divine spirit.

God is subtle but profound. It is not just that Jesus was a man with a life full of God. It is that the whole enterprise of history is God insinuating himself into the processes, the evidences, the data, the experiences of our material world. God is present everywhere. The entire universe is a world with a life full of God. Always in everything for those who have the eyes to see and ears to hear. We can all be persons with a life full of God. God is always personifying his grand and subtle nature in human persons, in human experience, in human perception. He enters even into the negatives of our lives and uses them as the very stuff out of which he makes constructive growth, seasoning, and deeply meaningful outcomes.

Five reasons why I believe in God! None of them is primarily about Jesus Christ. The reason to believe in Jesus Christ is that these five things compel us to believe in God. God's enterprise is always insinuating the divine spirit into all aspects of this world. So it is easy to understand that in Jesus the full thrust of the presence of God's spirit is evident to us, as Paul's says. The entire presence of the divine spirit is present in that one man, present in history, present in our lives.

Think again about John Paige's angel in the whirlwind. I was very pleased when one of our presidents, in his inaugural address said, "Never tiring, never yielding, never finishing, we renew that purpose of John Paige and Thomas Jefferson today to make our country more just and more generous." Because "The work continues, the story goes on. An angel still rides in the whirlwind. An angel still directs the storm." The Divine Spirit is persistently busy in our lives, teasing us out into our destiny of spiritual maturity. That makes sense to me. I believe in God. How can one ever not believe?

13

The Backside of God

INTRODUCTION

I SAID ABOVE THAT God is subtle. God is very hard to see. What *I* tried to make of my life did not pan out as I thought. Instead, what happened to me inadvertently, providentially shaped my destiny. I think it was never true that at the moment I was in the middle of the events of life I could see the providence of God's grace and guidance. I have only been able to see the golden thread of God's benevolent providence when I look back. Only then can I make sense out of what has unfolded. God is incredibly subtle in his presence to us in this world, and we see it only in retrospect.

It is probably a good thing that he is subtle. If God suddenly showed himself to us, plainly and unequivocally, every other day, once a week, once a year, or a couple of times in a lifetime, it might very well be counterproductive. We would most likely forget the content of the experience and concentrate instead upon the spectacular drama of the event. When I experience a dramatic event that seems to me to be "of the divine spirit," so to speak, I am usually thoroughly persuaded of it at the time. Then I spend the next six weeks rationalizing it away, as C. S. Lewis observed about his own experiences.

If God stepped out boldly and plainly before me, almost certainly I would wish to enshrine that time and place. Thereafter I would tend to be focused on the shrine where God had appeared. I would probably forget the meaning of God's appearance. I would certainly stop any further quest for experiencing God. That would be counterproductive. The Israelites of the Hebrew Bible always seemed to be playing around the edges of doing that very thing. So God was always busy destroying their shrines and idols, as he is always busy frustrating us in our efforts to concretize him. I wish God were more obvious. I long to satisfy the deep hunger in my soul with a surer sense of God. I would like to have a more tangible and palpable experience of God's presence. So would you.

Sometimes folks get the notion that humans might be able to capture God in theological constructs, well-defined and well-controlled. In all religious communities, unfortunately, we humans have made a major case out of getting God boxed up in our doctrines. Are we trying to keep God close or hold God at bay? Of course, humans are all tempted to try to throw some kind of a large interpretational net over God and to haul him into our own private or denominational worldview; or to expel him from existing at all.

Moses tried to haul God in. Read Exodus 33:12–23.

> Moses said to the LORD ... "I pray ... show me now your ways that I may know you ..." and [God] said, "My provident presence will go with you ..." [Moses] said to him, "If your provident presence will not go with us, do not bring us up from here into the promised land ..." And the LORD said to Moses, "I will do exactly this thing you have requested ..." Moses said, "... show me your glory (your true and full nature)." ... [God] said, "I will make all my goodness (provident presence) pass before you, and will proclaim before you my name, The LORD, ... but you cannot see my face (my full nature); a human cannot look me in the face and survive ... There is a place close to me, a rocky crest, where you may stand. While my provident presence passes by I will place you in a cleft in that rock, and I will cover you with my hand until I have passed by. Then I will take away my hand, and you shall see the shadow of my backside."

God is intentionally hard to see.

EXPLORING THE SUBTLETY

William James, the noted American psychologist of a hundred years ago, and Gordon Allport after him, said that there are two kinds of spirituality: extrinsic and intrinsic. Extrinsic spirituality is the sense of satisfying spiritual experience that we get from the projects, activities, worship events, and liturgies of our religion. These are the things we can act out in our religious practice. Some people find those completely satisfying and prefer them to intrinsic spirituality that has to do with the deep heartfelt inner sensations of hunger for God and communion with God that we feel in prayer, meditation, and other utterly personal worship experiences.

My father was quite an extrinsic Christian while my mother was more profoundly an intrinsic Christian. All of us extrinsic or intrinsic believers long everyday for a clearer, deeper, steadier, and better signal of God's presence. We would like a more certain trumpet, a more tangible experience of God's presence. But God does not give us much satisfaction on that. God is very subtle, extremely hard to see. I have really had to search God out; and I have had to spend a long time at it to make sure I had truly discerned that it was God I was experiencing. I had to develop the eyes to see and the ears to hear.

Moses was quite sure that he had seen God at the burning bush and he was certain he had gotten his commission right. So he went to Egypt and he did all of the things he was supposed to do to raise the revolution and lead the children of Israel out of Egypt. By the time of the story in Exodus 33 he had been leading them for a number of years. Then it came to him that he was not quite so sure as he had been about whether this really was God's project. He was not sure he had seen God since the burning bush, and that was a long time back. Was that really God he had heard from in that life-changing visitation in the Sinai? He was busy rationalizing away his spiritual mountain top experience, just as C. S. Lewis said he would. So he challenged God for being so subtle.

He said "I want to see your face. You've been lurking around the edges of our lives here for years—intimating that you are leading us somewhere, but we are not getting anywhere. In fact it looks like the children of Israel would rather worship a golden calf than keep up this subtle quest for your promised land. We want something tangible. We want some clear signal. We want a concrete God that we can experience. We are ready to cross the river Jordan and go into the promised land; but your promise now seems less and less clear, more and more uncertain. Your trumpet is muffled to the point I am not sure it is a trumpet call at all. It is very hard to see you. We cannot quite determine whether you are our projection of some kind of inner psychological wish, or a palpable spiritual reality. Have we created you in our own image out of our psychological perplexity? Are you really our perception of the real you, or our projection of a fanciful god? Show us your glory!"

The Backside of God

The Hebrew word used here for glory means "your whole nature, character, and operation." "Lay out before us once and for all the total picture of what in the world you are up to!" God replied to Moses in the story, "I will do what you ask. I will show myself to you; in fact I have already done so, but you cannot see my face, my full nature and work, and survive. If I showed you everything that I have been up to in the last 10,000 years, and particularly in the twentieth century, how I was present in the prosperity of your life and in the impairment of your child, in the death of your loved one, and in the rise of Hitler, Stalin, Saddam Hussein, and Osama bin Laden, and all the rest; if I gave you a snapshot of the total picture of how I am present in all of that "stuff" of history, it would be so overwhelming to you that you would not be able to come away with any kind of integrated sanity."

There is no suggesting in this passage that God causes any of the suffering and tragedy of life and history. It assures us, though, that he is present to it and not absent from it. "If I laid all of that before you in one presentation you would be distracted and overcome. Only I, God, can handle all the extremities of history and continue to function. I will show myself to you but you cannot look me full in the face. I will protect you in the cleft of the rock, and I will put my hand over you, and then I will pass by. After that I will take my hand away. You will see the shadow of my passing. You will see my backside." The Hebrew here is surprisingly crass. God said, "You will see my rearend!"

Moses wanted to see God face-to-face. So did Elijah. So did Isaiah. Isaiah said that in the year that King Uzziah died, he saw God in the temple and his *train* filled the temple, the *tail end* of God's regal robes. That is all that Isaiah got to see in his theophany: God's tail end. In his mythic story, Elijah thought he had seen God on Mt. Carmel when he had supernaturally defeated the prophets of Baal. It turns out, according to the angel that spoke to Elijah in that mythic story, that God does not live on Mt Carmel. He lives on Mt. Horeb. Elijah had a bad map. When Elijah went down to Jerusalem after the spectacular events on Mt. Carmel, nothing was happening to change things in Jerusalem.

So it was pretty clear to Elijah that God was not working at delivering God's people from persecution, giving them the true spirituality Elijah wanted for them. At least, it seemed to Elijah that if God was up to anything redemptive, he was very subtle and hard to see. So Elijah went to Mt. Horeb, as the angel suggested, and when he got there some dramatic things started to happen immediately. He thought God was in the earthquake which tore the mountain apart; but be was not in the earthquake. Elijah thought God was in the storm that followed, but he was not in the storm. He thought God was in the fire that exploded on the mountain top, and God was not in the fire. Then, when he was ready to give up again, Elijah discovered that God was in the still, small voice of subtle intimation that was whispering in Elijah's own mind and heart—in his third ear, as Reik would say.

That still small voice whispered to Elijah: "Get back Jerusalem. Stop goofing off up here on Mt. Horeb. You are wasting your time and my time trying to get me on the phone. Send me a fax and get back to work. There are 700 people in Jerusalem who have not bowed the knee to Baal. They are busy building my kingdom and you are lying around here feeling sorry for yourself. Stop looking for divine magic. While you have been out of commission I have knocked down two kings, set up two new ones, and appointed your successor, as well." God is usually awfully subtle. A quiet whisper in Elijah's subconscious is all he got, but it revealed God's truth and Elijah's destiny. Wow!

A PERSONAL JOURNEY TO THE BACKSIDE OF GOD

Six weeks after I retired from the United States Army at the beginning of 1990, I was recalled to active duty to field a plan I and my staff had written, for the mobilization of the special staff officers of the United States Army: Where could we get these people in the event of war? How were we going to man the slots available for them? How were we going to get enough slots for enough people? How were we going to fund them and train them? The Army gave me six weeks. I worked very hard for those six weeks. Working very late into the last night of my tour, I was putting the final touches to the program.

Suddenly there was a sharp lightening burst. It knocked out the power and wiped out my entire program of six weeks work. I gave up. I went to the BOQ and fell sound asleep, exhausted from the ardor and disappointment of the day. After a very short rest I awoke hearing the band play on the parade ground. It was introducing the retirement ceremony for a friend. I was supposed to give the opening prayer. I flung my body into the shower, stripped on my uniform, and ran across the parade ground. There were a lot of troops there doing PT. As I circled around them, I saw three young female solders, one of whom, was weeping heavily. I stopped and asked if I could help. One friend said, "Rachel is from a little town in Wisconsin, and she just got word that her girl friend committed suicide, the eighteenth suicide of a young woman in that town in 24 months.

The young soldier was devastated. I pointed out my office to her in the building across the street, told her to meet me there at 10 o'clock, and I would do what I could. After the parade, I met with her, and since I had to check out at noon, I referred her to one the permanent chaplains. She subsequently did well with the tragedy and grief. Now if my computer had not blown at two o'clock in the morning, I would not have gotten up late. I would not have been running across the parade ground. I would instead have been walking carefully and in a dignified way along the sidewalk, as a proper Army colonel should. I would not have encountered that young woman, and I would not have been able to intervene in her life. Was that an accident? Or was that serendipity? Or was that God's providence? God is not easy to see with certainty.

In the 1970s and 80s, I did a great deal of research work in South Africa. One autumn I had to go to South Africa to give a series of lectures. I flew to New York, lay over there a couple of hours, and proceeded to board the plane for Johannesburg. The woman processing the loading of the flight stopped me. She looked at my visa and said "I'm sorry I cannot let you board. Your visa is not correct." I said "It must be correct, I have spent weeks making certain that everything is just right." "No it is not" She replied. "You must go to the consulate in the city and get it corrected. If I let you board the plane the government will fine the airline $10,000."

I had a deadline for lecturing and preaching that weekend in South Africa, and of course South African flights usually only fly from New York every other day. I quickly went downtown to the consulate and turned in my passport and visa. However, it was delayed and the consulate indicated they could not solve the problem in time.

I was walking out of the lobby, all forlorn, when I ran into an old friend from the Chicago consulate. He was now the Vice Consul in New York. He could get anything done that he wanted done. So in about ten minutes he had resolved all visa and passport problems and had me booked on the next plane.

I went back to the airport early in the morning and was informed that the plane would be two hours late. There was virtually no one in the airport, except the woman who had previously thrown me off the plane. She hailed me and said "Yesterday you gave me your card that says you are the Executive Director of the Christian Association for Psychological Studies. What is this business of Christian and Psychology?"

I said, "Well, that is what I do." She said, "I need your help. For twenty years I have had an excellent job with the airline. I own a magnificent apartment in Manhattan and collect art from all over the world. I have a beautiful life. I fly anywhere I want to go. I take vacations in the most exotic places—but every morning when I get up I want to kill myself. I was born from an American solder and a Dutch woman, abandoned at birth, lived in orphanages until I was 16, and was repeatedly sexually abused. Finally, in a rage I ran away, went to a distant city, and I signed up at a university. Now I speak seven languages, have a master's degree, and I am able to achieve what I want in my life. Every morning I feel like killing myself." I said "How old are you?" She said "48."

I continued my conversation with her for two hours until I boarded the plane. Then I assured her I would correspond with her and I would not give up on her until we had found a solution. We carried on this correspondence for about a half year. Meanwhile, I referred her to a friend, a psychiatrist in New York, who treated her very successfully for the diagnosis that I had given her, namely, severe depression and paranoia associated with menopause. It was a matter of bio-chemistry. She was short on estrogen. When she received the medical supplements and appropriate supportive care, she did very well, despite her early life trauma. Now she has her wonderful life back. What messed up my visa? Was that an accident, serendipity, or providence? I think I see a shadow of the divine in it, in retrospect.

Moses was really confused by this kind of stuff. So am I. So are you. I want to see God face-to-face. I want a clearer signal. I want to have deep and profound assurances of God's presence. I want the eyes to see, the ears to hear. I am willing to live as a pilgrim, to take days one at a time, to keep an open ended quest for truth and insight. I am ready to pay that price if I can just see God. But God says, "You cannot see me that clearly. It would be too weighty for you. But I will tell you what I will do—when the storms of life rage over you, there is a place near me, a cleft in the rock. I will hold you in the cleft of the rock, and I will put my hand over you, and then the full force of life can pass by. I will pass through your life with all of the power, mystery, and awesomeness of my nature. Then

I will take my hand away and if you have the eyes to see and the ears to hear, you will see the shadow of my backside."

When I was five years old, I was madly in love with Esther Van Houten. Esther was also five. She lived in the farmstead across the country road from ours. We talked that summer of 1937 about starting school together in September. We were very excited. We were very happy. We were very much in love. The summer was bright and beautiful for two innocent kids. I remember the wonderful days of sunshine. I am sure there were days of rain, but I do not remember them.

Esther was five in April. I was five in July. On the third of August, I was standing next to the well outside of our farm home. I remember seeing vaguely the image of my mother through the kitchen window. It was a brilliant day of warm sun. I am not quite sure what I was thinking, but I remember I was lost in thought when I heard the Van Houten's screen door slam. My heart leaped at the thought of running over to play with Esther. I looked up to see her. There she stood, at the top of the driveway, completely on fire, and she burned to death right there before my face. I screamed for my mother, but we could not save her.

That was the end of my life. I have no recollection from that day until I was seven. Esther's death changed everything for me. I have no idea now who I was before her death. I cannot recover the memory of what kind of person I was then or might have been had she lived and we had continued our joy. A blackness came down over me that night when my mother told me Esther was dead. It did not lift until I was seven. I have no memory of those two black years.

Then one day in July of 1939, I stepped out of the horse barn into the bright summer sun and was immediately irradiated with a sense of the Divine Spirit filling every corpuscle of my body and soul. I was immediately saturated with a sense of joy and meaning and light. In that moment the two years of darkness were taken away from me miraculously. I did not throw them off by reason of some new insight. They were taken away. I felt like I was caught up in an intense cone of light that reached out from some place infinitely above me. I was filled with a sense of transcendence—of being lifted up above all the suffering and pain of life—not just my life but of life.

That filled me with a pervasive sense of meaning. I was filled with an awareness that my life could be exciting and its meaning would be experienced in finding the way to help all the suffering people around me.

The two years of darkness had taken me through the depths of the Great Depression, and for some reason children were dying everywhere in our little immigrant community. Suddenly the burden of being weighed down by all the anguish was removed and replaced with a sense of empowerment, purpose, and joy. An incredible lightness of being seemed to lift me above it all and turn the future into a clear way forward, an open vista of brilliance and meaning.

The minister in our community was the only person who seemed to have any power to do anything about the community's suffering, the only one from outside of our little Dutch rural ghetto that stood above the anguish and trauma of those years. He was the only model that seemed empowered to help humans. I sensed that my destiny was to follow him, to do what he did.

Esther's death changed my life. Everything from that day on has been radically different from what it would ever have been, I am sure. Everything that is important or meaningful about me is a result of her death. My life has been a straight line from August 3, 1937, to this moment. I never had any inclination to turn aside from that destiny. I am here today writing these words because Esther burned to death in front of my face, and I was helpless to do anything about it. Of course I have grieved it every day since. It has forged both my personality pathologies and my creative strengths. Her death has shaped my destiny in detail. Was that an accident? Or serendipity? Or providence? It seems almost obscene to me to ask that question. I can do it only with surges of utter grief.

CONCLUSION

God is so subtle, but just when I would write him off, there comes soaking into my brain and heart the penetrating awareness, from which I cannot extricate myself, that God did not kill Esther Van Houten; but God entered into it. Somehow God was there. What came of it had everything in the world to do with God's presence in it and in me. It changed me completely and forged my life of ministry, despite the perpetual pain. I really wish I had Esther back, and many days of my life I cannot wait to see her again, as I know I will.

God did not foul up my visa to South Africa but he used it to save the life of a creative woman who had been badly abused by life. My inadvertency gave back to her a life of joy and meaning. God did not glitch my army computer, but he was not absent from it; and he had in mind a suffering waif of a little girl from a small Wisconsin town. Because I was just there, just then, God gave her growth and meaning from her pain.

In a subtle whisper God was there—and, my friends, I saw him. I look back and still I see the shadow of his passing. God does not cause the suffering and tragedy in life, but God is not absent from any moment of it. In fact the only thing that makes any sense at all of my whole life—and world—is the fact that in just that kind of way, God has been traversing my life for all these seventy-eight years. God is subtle, indeed, but his presence and providence is the surest fact of my life experience.

PART THREE

How the Divine Spirit Really Works in the Church

14

Healthy Faith Needs Good Theology

WHEN WE EXPLORE THE meaning of Jesus' and Paul's personal trust in an all-forgiving God, we immediately find ourselves in a complex process. So many voices have tried to explain that trust and God's unconditional forgiveness since Jesus' day. The history of the Christian Church since Jesus time is, at best, a variegated stream of many interpretations, and at worst a swamp of opposite and confusing messages. Indeed, even in the OT and NT themselves, there is a panoply of amazingly different ways of understanding the God that Jesus trusted.

For much of the last 4,000 years God has been portrayed in a way that would force one to conclude that God is critically ill. If you take seriously what most people have believed about God for the last four millennia, you must conclude that he is badly in need of a psychotherapist. That is, in most faith traditions the reports on God's nature and function indicate that his patterns of relationality, affect, and ideation have been outside of normal range. To be very specific, in many folks' view God apparently suffers from chronic paranoid schizophrenia, or severe Borderline Personality Disorder, with frequent erratic, unprovoked episodes of active psychosis.

Now this sounds strange, but let me explain. The dominant stream of reports on God that make up the theology of most faith traditions indicates that God operates with the psychotic notion that he is caught in a cosmic battle with another "god" who threatens to thwart, corrupt, and undo his work. This is a classic psychotic syndrome in that, according to the reports, it forms a global ideation shaping God's entire worldview. However, there is no empirical, heuristic, or phenomenological evidence to indicate that any such cosmic conflict or evil reality exists.

In such faith traditions, God's *notion* of reality has no actual reality to which it corresponds. When we find this in humans we call it insanity. Moreover, this pattern of ideation is specifically paranoid since it indicates that God thinks there are forces out there that are out to get him, whereas there exists no evidence that such forces exist. If these faith tradition reports about him or views of him are accurate, these notions are figments of God's sick imagination. Such a God is insane. The God of ancient Israelite religion, described in the OT, from which came Judaism, Christianity, and Islam, is diagnosably ill.

Sick Gods make for sick people. To put it slightly differently, sick Gods make people sick. Just as children and disciples model their parents and mentors, so individuals and communities of humans create themselves in the images of their gods. Sick Gods provide sick models which produce sick persons and sick communities. To insure personal and communal wellbeing requires that one's God is well; or at least the converse is so. If one's God is sick one cannot achieve wellbeing, individually or communally.

Now you may feel that somehow I am too severe in my clinical diagnosis of the kind of God in which a lot of people believe. So let me recite a more palpable panoply of symptoms which, according to the dominant attitudes in many faith traditions, constitute the syndrome of God's clinical disorder. God is reported by many folks to suffer from a perfectionistic need to have the world, and all who happen to wander through it, carefully conform to a prescribed set of thought forms and behavior. This sounds rather obsessive-compulsive, to say the least; particularly when you consider that the world he created is not a production factory or forced labor camp; but is designed by God to be more like a greenhouse in which the primary style and objective is that of growth and development. That necessitates a constant process of experimentation, change, and unpredictability.

Perhaps you have not taken these reports of his demand for conformity so seriously as to have been much affected by this pathological symptom. But what about the fact that it is reported that God is so ticked off about human nature and behavior, human exploration and experimentation, that he simply cannot get his head screwed back on right until he has literally killed somebody.

Take, for example, the drowning of all of Noah's community; or killing Onan and his brother for refusing to marry a woman who was obviously severely problematic in the first place; or the drowning of the Egyptian army at the Red Sea. Or think of God's threatened genocide of the Israelites at Mount Sinai; the actual genocide of the Canaanites during the Israelite invasion and outright theft of their land; the extermination of the northern Israelite kingdom by sending the Assyrian invasion, according to the Bible story; the exile of thousands from Judah to Babylon for seventy years; the sudden death of the man who tried to protect the Ark of the Covenant from falling into the mud; and the incineration of Sodom and Gomorrah for failing to be hospitable to strangers.

Now if this does not sound to you like a pattern of consummate narcissism, chronic situation-inappropriateness, sadistic vindictiveness, impulsiveness and Obsessive Compulsive Disorder, depressive and irrational rage, being out of touch with reality and reacting in ways that are out of proportion to the actual problematic events at hand in each case; you have not been paying attention. At least you have not been reading your Bible regularly. The behavioral syndrome I have just laid out is flagrant psychosis.

Moreover, what about the fact that his furor was so intense toward you and me, according to the New Testament, innocent as we are, that he either had to exterminate us or slaughter his unique Son, Jesus of Nazareth. If these reports are true, this God is one sick puppy, and dangerous. He solves all his ultimate impasses with ultimate violence. Don't you think that is sick? Any God is a monster if he cannot behave at least as well as the average human in his or her better moments would like to behave. Monster gods make monster people.

I referred to us as innocent. You may disagree. I concede that the only evil which exists in our world is the evil we do to each other. We are all guilty of that and ought to be ashamed of ourselves. When I claim innocence, however, I mean to call attention to the fact that we humans did not ask to be born. We did not ask to be limited. We did not ask to be flawed. We did not ask to be developmental and therefore inherently and inevitably incomplete, growing, changing, achieving by trial and error, experimenting, exploring, and sometimes running down dead-end streets morally, relationally, psychological, and spiritually. We did not ask to be floated upon the ocean of time and space with an inadequate database, immature judgment, and emotions often driven by anxiety about it all. We did not ask to be assigned a *divine task* of making sense of and finding meaning in this world, while being compelled to operate with mere *human resources*.

The worst of all this is that religious metaphors that we have been given in the dominant report from the OT about God's nature and behavior, produce unconscious psychological archetypes in human beings. These get acted out unsuspectingly in behavior that is justified by those metaphors. If God solves all his ultimate problems by quick resort to ultimate violence, how is it possible that we can expect humans to do significantly differently? Sick gods make sick people. If God persuades us of his psychotic notion that he is caught in a cosmic conflict, the battle ground of which is human history and the human heart, of course it is inevitable that we shall wish, unconsciously or consciously, to help him out; to be on his side in the war; to undertake God's cause against the infidel, to fight the bad guys, to exterminate our enemies, as apparently God tries to do with his.

This is the flag under which ancient Israelite campaigns were fought against the Canaanites and one often wonders about Israeli campaigns today against the Palestinians and anybody else who looks cross-eyed at Israel—they even bombed and torpedoed a U.S. ship that was not where they liked to have it. This is the flag under which the Christian campaigns of the Crusades were fought and one often wonders about the right-wing Christian crusades today, especially Christian Zionism. This is the flag under which Islam conquered the Mediterranean world in the seventh and eighth centuries and it is clear that one need not wonder at all about the al-Qaeda ambitions today. A sick God produces sick people. How shall we achieve wellbeing if our God is so sick? We shall not, under any circumstances!

There was, of course, another report on God's mental health in the OT and NT, though it has been heavily discounted throughout history, often to the point of scoffing disbelief. It is the claim that the dominant report of God as psychotic, which has always been everywhere afloat, has nothing to do with God at all, but is instead the sick projection of a lot of untutored human imaginations—projected by people scared to death of the unknown and the unpredictable in life. Such views of God are mere projections of human terrors upon the human idealized mental image of the imagined mentor those people thought was God.

The second report on God's mental health has had a hard time competing with that sick dominant report, even though all the biblical and experiential evidence is everywhere confirming this alternative report. This alternative report has been resisted because it seems so humanly unbelievable, because it claims that God is a God of unconditional grace to all humankind, in spite of our human limitations and dead end streets.

Carl Rogers did not think it was an inherently unbelievable idea that humans could exercise unconditional positive regard for each other, even if it often seems very rare and rather unnatural. But even he was most hesitant to believe it true of God. He said he abandoned his fundamentalist evangelical roots because the dominant report of a faith tradition in which God seemed insane was endemic to any religious thought, as he saw it. Thus, he could preach human unconditional grace, but could not imagine unconditional grace in God. He just could not wrap his head around Genesis 12 and 17, and Abraham's breakthrough insight that God really is trying to get across to the human race: "I am announcing to you that I will be a God to you and to your children after you, throughout their generations, for an everlasting covenant, no strings attached. You will be my people and I will be your God, and that is all there is to it."

Carl Rogers could not repress the dominant report ringing in his ears, despite the fact that it was a false report. He could not hear the strains of that grace refrain playing all the way through the Old and New Testament, declaring as did the prophet Micah (7:18–20), "Who is a God like our God. He pardons iniquity. He passes over transgression. He will not be angry forever. He delights in steadfast love. He will have compassion on us. He is faithful to us when we are unfaithful to him. He tramples our iniquities under his feet, and casts all our sins into the sea of his eternal forgetfulness. Moreover, he guaranteed to us that we are forgiven before we were born and before we could imagine how to be clever sinners." Unfortunately, Carl Rogers is joined by much of the human race throughout history, who cannot imagine that God is not a god of terror and threat. Cannot imagine that St. Paul knew something essential about God's nature and behavior when he declared doxologically, "I am persuaded that nothing in all God's creation can separate us from the love of God" (Romans 8:28).

Now, that is a fairly healthy God. God, the warrior, the vindictive judge, the impulsive slayer, the genocidal maniac, is a monster and nobody should honor him. He makes me sick! He makes us all sick. God, the purveyor of unconditional grace is situation-appropriate, a key gradient of good mental health. We are human, we did not ask to be human, to be born, to be limited in our data base, to be creatures of growth and change, to be unfolding persons that inherently need to explore and experiment and imagine by trial and error.

We did not ask for our transcendental task and our mere mundane resources. Any God who does not see that and respond with unconditional positive regard is a very sick monster. That is why John says that the real God is *faithful and just to forgive us!* (1 John 1:9). Did you hear that? It is a matter of justice that for the likes of us, caught in our limited humanness, the only right thing is mercy. "As a father pities his children so God pities us who contemplate him as awesome!" (Psalm 103:9). Now that is a *healthy* God. Healthy people are, therefore, awestruck by such a God. Who is a God like our God?

15

Wellbeing

God's Grace and Human Health

SENSIBLE PEOPLE ARE ALL motivated to be the kind of healthy humans who perceive that God is healthy and a God of utter grace, are we not? That perspective insinuates into our minds and hearts the sense that the Holy Spirit of God is every where in our lives manifesting God's self. Most every decent human is interested in human wellbeing—indeed, in the wellbeing of the entire cosmos. The health and wellbeing of the universe, of course, depends very largely upon how well we look after human wellbeing.

I have argued in the previous chapter that our wellbeing depends directly upon our perception of God's wellbeing. That is, we are addressing the problem of God's Health and Human Health, which I have translated into the issue of God's Grace and Human Health. What can we do to insure that the report on God's nature and behavior tells the story of his robust health and inherent good will toward us; thereby insuring that our base of operations and our basic assumptions will enhance human wellbeing? How can we make sure that our perception of God is not instead the universally dominant lie that he is a monster?

To put the question in a more operationally clinical and scientific form: How can we bring good theology and responsible psychology into the kind of authentic interface that they mutually illumine each other so as to enlighten our interpretation of human nature? Gerkin calls this quest to understand human nature the study of The Living Human Document.[1] How can we do this in such a fashion as to indicate what will produce our true wellbeing in body, mind, and soul? What can make

---

1. Charles V. Gerkin, *The Living Human Document: Re-visioning Pastoral Counseling in a Hermeneutical Mode* (Nashville: Abingdon, 1984).

us well materially and economically, intellectually, aesthetically, and spiritually?

I am thoroughly persuaded that psychology and spirituality are two terms for the same domain. Each has its own universe of discourse and, therefore, its own *modus operandi*; but the domains of psychology and spirituality are the same: the complex panoply of critical aspects shaping the irrepressible human quest for earthly and heavenly meaning.

Any psychologist who does not take seriously the light that human spirituality can bring to bear upon the scientific discipline of psychology is simply not truly serious about his or her own profession or his or her own psychology. Any theologian who does not take seriously the light that human psychology can bring to bear upon the scientific discipline of theology is simply not truly serious about his or her own theological profession, nor his or her own personal spirituality.

The sciences of psychology and theology, done properly and responsibly, inevitably interface at four scientific levels: theory development, research models, data management, and clinical application. At each of those levels, it is in the model of human nature that is forming and functioning there, that psychology and theology interface. Each brings to bear its distinct light for the illumination of the real and comprehensive understanding of the Living Human Document. Human persons are after all the subject of the scientific work of both theology and psychology. Moreover, within that human model to which both psychology and spirituality, or its scientific instrument, theology, contribute, it is the personality theory forming and functioning there that is the central site of the mutual illumination the two sciences provide each other.

An illustration of what this means and how this works might be developed upon the basis of an ancient biblical story that, in its historic reading has seemed to report that God is sick, establishing a religious metaphor that has produced really sick human archetypes and sick humans for 3,000 years. That is the story in Genesis 3 about the fall of Adam and Eve, their expulsion from the idyllic world of Eden, and their being cursed by God.

There is another way to read this story. As it stands, it is a rewrite in Hebrew language of a much more ancient Mesopotamian fertility myth. There is the fruitful tree, the virgin seducing and being seduced, the phallic symbol of the snake, and the triple seduction: the snake and Eve mutually seducing each other and Eve's seduction of Adam. Read literally, in terms of long theological traditions, this is a relatively superficial report that our first parents disobeyed a specific arbitrary divine command. God got mad, threw them out of Paradise, and cursed. That is the monster God.

If one asks why the ancient Hebrews liked this story and adopted it, the answer is obvious. They had a monster God. They experienced the world as profoundly troubled and in trouble. They had the option of accusing God of having created it that way, as they did in their older narrative in Genesis 6, or of letting God off the hook by accusing themselves, as they do in Genesis 3. The one truth they knew in it all was that anyone reading the story immediately acknowledges that it describes our real-life experience. Life is troubled. We feel inadequate and ashamed about that. We long for love and meaning. We are very anxious about our sexuality and spirituality. We feel cast out of or alienated from our true destiny. We long for our father but cannot seem to catch hold of his hand. They knew the story somehow rang true to some of our worst perplexities. We are lost souls and at a loss. They did not know that there was another way to read it.

They assumed the dominant story about a threatening God was the true model of reality. However, if we bring the other report to bear on this story, the report of God as a God of grace that is unconditional, radical, and universal; and illumine the fall story with a sound psychological perspective, it is readily evident that this is a story about the inevitable adolescence of the human race. It is a story about leaving the womb and the nursery, exploring the possibilities of our own personhood, individuating ourselves from parental authority, discovering the knowledge of our potential for good and for evil, and disclosing to ourselves the meaning of our sexuality, spirituality, and individuation.

With the mutual illumination of sound psychology and good theology, this story becomes the poetic suggestion that Adam and Eve needed to assert their individuality against the constraints of parental authority, even divine authority, in order to find their true selves. The enigma in the narrative of Genesis 3 is in the realization that the fall was a necessary act of growth, and raises the question as to whether that adolescent process for persons and communities is best achieved by evolution or revolution.

Adam and Eve chose revolution. The narrative, properly illumined by good theology and good psychology, is not a story about God cursing them for that. It is a narrative about living with the inevitable consequences of the necessary and unavoidable choices that growth requires. The chief human choices in life and growth must always be made without adequate knowledge of the future, without adequate insight about our options and alternatives, and without sufficient knowledge of the ambiguity of adult responsibility. God's remarks upon Adam's and Eve's escape from infancy, and from the Edenic nursery are not a curse prescribed by a God of threat and vengeance, but a destiny described by a God of grace, namely, the picture of responsible adult life as painful hard work!

An appropriate psycho-spiritual illumination of our metaphors, and the archetypes they produce, can afford us a healthy God who inspires healthy people. I mean this, not as a liturgical litany. I mean it as a clinically operational fact. Human wellbeing depends upon good theology and sound psychology producing wholesome and whole spirituality. Here I mean spirituality not as a mere transcendental myth. I mean it as the function and experience of the inner person, in the quest that a person pursues, to be thoroughly infused with the cadences of the poetry and music of truly gratifying *meaning* in life. I mean a kind of wellbeing that is that wholeness of personhood and community, which derives from a comprehensive and satisfying sense of the meaningfulness of life, individually and in relationship. Our spirituality is the universal and irrepressible human hunger for meaning, earthly and heavenly.

This is possible for us all and for all humanity: for you and me, George Bush, al-Qaeda, the Democrats, even the French! Though, of course, that 15% of every human community that suffers from inherited severe borderline syndrome or psychosis cannot achieve this, except with appropriate medication. As humans, it is imperative that we develop a psycho-spiritual strategy, with an attendant psycho-social program of operation, that reflects a thoroughgoing grace perspective. This outlook and style of unconditional positive regard for one-another needs to be carried out against the backdrop of the conviction that such an unconditional grace posture is the real model in God, as well.

Such a posture has a chance to so shape our assumptions about personality development and about human nature that a new global model of constructive relationality can be fashioned between persons, communities, and nations. This is essential to human wellbeing and without it we will continue down the trajectory of ever increasing levels of violence.

It must be grounded in a wholesome psycho-spiritual model. The Islamic fundamentalists have finally done us a great favor: namely, to pitch to us the clear signal that what shapes human meaning is the issue of whether God is sick or well. Their God is very sick, insane; but then it is not very different than the gods perceived and worshipped by the Western world for three or four millennia.

This psycho-spiritually honest way of reading the God story acknowledges that the problem of human un-wellbeing, human dysfunction, is not the problem of sin, in the modern moralistic construction of that concept, but the problem of sickness, human inadequacy and incompleteness in the face of the responsibilities of life and the challenges of godliness. We fall short of the mark—of our own and God's ideals for us because we were created as limited humans.

An operational model of a wholesome and healing kind of personal and global relationality has at least the following ten practical characteristics. First, the incarnation of a grace perspective within the personality of every one who cares about this. That means a new initiative of unconditional acceptance of the adversary or diverse other. Such acceptance means cherishing every human being just where each person or community is at this moment in his or her psycho-spiritual health or malignancy.

Second, such a healing model requires a profound empathy that places the one who cares within the frame of reference of the diverse or alienated other person or community (read al Qaeda, for example). This will lead the caring person to discern the sources and nature of the obstructions to grace-filled relationality suffered by the diverse other. It will also suggest possibilities for overcoming that alienation. Such unconditional grace affords the alienated person or community the potential for a new sense of self-worth, wholesome meaning, and a healthy God-story.

Third, this initiative provides both persons and communities a sense of mutuality in the quest for wellbeing. Fourth, it implies an acknowledgment that the caring initiator comes to the relationship with human impairments as well as does the diverse or alienated "enemy."

Fifth, in this context, there is a chance for it to become evident that the caring person's or community's world view expresses a comprehensive ambition for the wholeness of the whole world of humans and things. This clarifies the fact that the diverse other's wellbeing is genuinely sought for in that setting. Sixth, this should make apparent that the mutual growth of both persons and communities is a real and expected possibility and the true desire on the part of the caring initiator.

Seventh, both may then come to realize operationally the extent to which human wellbeing depends upon the health of the God each envisions. Islam has long centuries of such a view of Allah as prompted a richly wholesome culture and relationality with Jews and Christians. The Medieval Spanish Islamic society, under its independent Caliphate, was a reasonably admirable example of such grace. It would be great to see that again in Islam.

Eighth, it may be anticipated that this strategy will evoke such a level of security and trust that it can set aside defensive patterns on both sides. That would have a chance to defeat obstructions to mutuality, growth, wholeness, and wellbeing. Ninth, both persons and communities might then realize that they are being taken seriously and affirmed.

Tenth, the effectiveness of this journey into unconditional positive regard could be measured and critiqued psycho-spiritually at each step along the way. The standard of measurement and criteria would be the expectation that the ultimate achievement of mutual wellbeing will be realized as psycho-spiritual maturity. This would likely bring with it the benefits, materially, economically, intellectually, aesthetically, and spiritually, that represent true wholeness.

The Diverse Others of which I speak above may be relatively benign colleagues in a vigorous dialogue in which significant polarity is evident between the views presented. They may be lethal opponents in military, political, and cultural crises, such as that between al-Qaeda and the U.S. today. In the latter case, particularly as it applies to al-Qaeda, the diversity and lethality may be driven by one or more of the following dynamics. First, it may be that the adversary is afflicted with psychosis. If that is what we are up against in this case, mere dialogue and negotiation will get us nowhere. Only medication of such pathological persons works to produce the constructive management of the symptoms necessary to make mutuality possible. Short of proper medication the only course of action is the tough love of forcefully imposing such boundaries upon them as prevents them from perpetrating mayhem upon society or themselves.

Alternatively, the motive may be a legitimate socio-political objective of preserving the Umma, Islamic domain, from incursions and erosions due to Western military or commercial-industrial interests; and the unwelcome, society-opening influences that always accompany such incursions.

Thirdly, al-Qaeda may be motivated by legitimate anguish and fear regarding the trivialization of Islam's spiritual-cultural ideals and values through the offensive, devaluing impact upon Islamic culture and spirituality that comes from Western cultural artifacts and the values those imply. If I were a spiritually intense and devoted Muslim, however gracious and grace-filled, I would be immensely angry about the incursions into my world of the current popular Western music, Hollywood films that seem to champion the sick side of human life, and Disney videos that are now rife with violence and mayhem.

I am very angry, myself, that I need to put up with all that constantly in my own home culture in America. The artifacts of Western culture today are largely superficial and trivializing, fraught with sick values and ideals, cluttered with images that erode ones sense of gentlemanliness and decency. They degrade human dignity and idealism in thought and behavior. Why would Islam not be thoroughly enraged by the poisoning of its culture with our corrosive malignancies? It is an enormous tragedy for the entire world that American values and daily experience are now so dominated by the ignorant, undereducated, superficial, and trivializing minds that populate Hollywood and the entertainment scene generally.

Moreover, why do we think we must deliver Muslim women from wearing the Islamic clothing that covers their bodies? For many of them, I am told, wearing such clothing is an expression of their own inner desire for dignity, for inner peace, and for spiritual integrity. It is their way of freeing themselves from the distractions of the body and materiality, releasing them to center on their life in the spirit. That is an ideal to be endorsed, even though it would be difficult today to find an American under thirty who would understand my saying that.

Is there not some reason to endorse the desire for chaste dignity on the part of Muslim women, assuming it is their own choice? Is that not infinitely better than the behavior of American fifteen-year-old children whose parents bring them to my clinic for treatment because they have been high on pot, behaving illicitly and self-destructively? Not that I think virginity is a prize or sexual experimentation is evil. I mean that the Hollywood dominant culture that promotes mindless promiscuity among the young before than can possibly know what they are doing and what it means, is sick. The desire to be wiser and more decent is healthier. If that is what Muslim women seek with their unique coverings, bless them.

The present world conflict which has taken the form of international violence and terrorism is the currently most dangerous threat to human wellbeing. This danger is accompanied by the terrifying advance of AIDS and the waste of resources that might be invested in enhancing advances in medicine, mental health, education, and the creation of a culture of aesthetics in our world. All these terrors continue to violate and erode human wellbeing because our unconscious and conscious psycho-spiritual models and archetypes are largely formed along the axis of the sick side of the message of the Hebrew Bible. That message is one of vindictiveness, quid-pro-quo strategies of settling scores, imposing arbitrary boundaries upon persons and communities by forcing discipline upon them, meeting force with force, doing unto others what we would not have them do unto us, and making sure, under the doctrine of preemptive defense, that we do it to them first.

These archetypes of fighting fire with fire are products of unconscious metaphors that contend that the world is wired this way, the cosmos is wired this way, God is wired this way. Everything is wired for a cosmic conflict. Have you got a major problem, resort to ultimate force. God does. Why should not we? It's how things are designed. God was so ticked off at us that he could not get his head screwed back on straight until he had killed somebody, us or his unique son, that rather nice guy from Nazareth. That's the familiar way things are set up. It is not the way of the Divine Spirit.

Anton Boisen, Seward Hiltner,[2] and Donald Capps[3] proposed a trajectory of modifying the inner person by reframing the models of external behavior. They hoped that would produce eventual inner change.

---

2. LeRoy Aden and J. Harold Ellens, eds., *Turning Points in Pastoral Care: The Legacy of Anton Boisen and Seward Hiltner* (Grand Rapids: Baker, 1990).

3. Donald Capps and Janet L. Jacobs, eds., *The Struggle for Life, A Companion to William James's* The Varieties of Religious Experience, SSSR Monograph Series 9 (West Lafayette, IN: Society for the Scientific Study of Religion, 1995). See also Robert J. Wicks, Richard D. Parsons, and Donald Capps, *Clinical Handbook of Pastoral Counseling*, 2 vols., Integration Books (New York: Paulist, 1993).

John Carter, Bruce Narramore,[4] and H. Newton Malony[5] urged a reform of our inner function by restructuring the human moral framework with a combination of rather literal biblical theology and psychodynamic psychology. They thought the *oughts and shoulds* of the disciplinary God-tradition would do it. Sigmund Freud[6] and Carl Jung[7] thought, and Eugen Drewermann[8] thinks psychoanalytic psychology can re-channel the function of our unconscious archetypes.

The works of all of these have their uses; but they do not reach the deep structure challenges where the real work needs to be done. They are not the expressions of the essential nature and work of God's pervasive spirit in the world and in human persons. Al-Qaeda will continue to find ways to fight for Allah as long as the belief persists that Allah is a God of jihad and fatwah, for exterminating infidels in the Muslim Umma. This is no different than the Christian enterprise of the Crusades of the twelfth century CE, and their Warrior God who intended for his minions "to deliver the Holy Places from the infidel Turk." One wonders about present-day crusading spirits. This is not different than the Israelite conviction that they engaged in ethnic cleansing of Canaan in the twelfth century BCE, because that was the mandate of God. It makes one startle to realize that the modern-day Israelis thought up the current wicked notion of preemptive defense and seem busy with the ethnic cleansing of East Jerusalem and the West Bank by making it illegal or intolerable for Palestinians to live there.[9]

---

4. John D. Carter and Bruce Narramore, *The Integration of Psychology and Theology: An Introduction* (Grand Rapids: Zondervan, 1979). See also J. Harold Ellens, *God's Grace and Human Health* (Nashville: Abingdon, 1982).

5. H. Newton Malony, ed., *Current Perspectives in the Psychology of Religion* (Grand Rapids: Eerdmans, 1977). See also Malony, ed., *A Christian Existential Psychology: The Contributions of John G. Finch* (Lanham, MD: University Press of America, 1980).

6. Sigmund Freud, *Selected Writings* (New York: Book-of-the-Month Club, 1997).

7. Carl Gustav Jung, ed., *Selected Writings* (New York: Book-of-the-Month Club, 1997). See also Jung, *Man and His Symbols* (Garden City, NY: Doubleday, 1964).

8. Matthias Beier, *A Violent God-Image: An Introduction to the Work of Eugen Drewermann* (New York: Continuum, 2004).

9. J. Harold Ellens, *The Destructive Power of Religion, Violence in Judaism, Christianity, and Islam, Condensed and Updated Edition* (Westport, CT: Praeger, 2007).

CONCLUSION

I do not mean to propose here any kind of soft-headed trivialization of the problem of human dysfunction by seeming to psychologize or spiritualize it in a Sunday School kind of superficiality. Neither do I underestimate the size of the challenge. I intend my proposal to be closer to the hard-headed aggressive rationalism of Ayn Rand than to the manipulative sentimentality of contentious, soft-headed American liberalism.

We will not achieve human wellbeing until we create a world culture of wellbeing. We shall not achieve that until God gets well in our theological constucts. A world culture of wellbeing implies a world of psycho-spiritual metaphors that produce healthful unconscious archetypes. To achieve that we must destroy the sick monster God that reigns unconsciously in all our hearts. Furthermore, we must train our children for that in every new generation. The programs of psychological and moral reframing are worth the trouble. Freud and Jung have given us much help. But it is the monster God that sometimes appears in the Hebrew Bible (OT) that must be exorcised and killed, if we are to achieve some gains toward the world of wellbeing we can imagine, instead of the lethal world we continually tend to create.

Judaism, Christianity, and Islam must rediscover the God of grace and then learn to care about behaving in that same grace. Short of that we will continue to stumble along in our self-constructed hell of violence, degradation, and death: spiritually, psychologically, aesthetically, culturally, economically, and socially. Sick gods make sick people. Healthy theology has a chance to make humans wholesome and healthy. The quality of our faith traditions is the key. Our wills are free within the bounds of that to which our hearts are committed, should I say, addicted.

16

Responsible Religion, Honest Theology, Good Grace

INTRODUCTION

THE CHAPTERS OF THIS volume do not apologize for implying a deep appreciation for the central theme of the Bible, and a critical view of the creeds and traditions of the church. Rather, they are intended as an honest way to promote responsible religion, authentic theology, and good grace. Of course, when one uses terms like that one has a responsibility to say something about what they mean. When I say that these chapters intended to urge responsible religion, I mean that they were designed to invite us to take a view of the Bible that cuts through our tendencies toward traditional dogma and inflexible attitudes in handling the quest of the Bible itself. This book has invited us, rather, to explore and express spiritually healthful notions about how God is in this world, what he is or can be to us, and what we can know about that from the Bible, rather than from our creeds and theological dogma.

Truth is always openended, and thus religion must always be a developing quest, not a closed system of propositional theology or traditional interpretations of sacred scriptures. When institutional religion or theological traditions become closed systems they kill spiritual vitality and the spiritual quest for growth and understanding. Humans have always been tempted to define God in our own private way and we often feel that we have God packaged and could pop him into our vest pockets and keep him static and under control. John Cobb and others, particularly scholars in the Process Theology traditions have helped us understand how dynamic God is and how interactive he means to be with us.[1] It is humbling and hope-inducing to discover that we cannot

---

1. John B. Cobb Jr. and David Ray Griffin, *Process Theology: An Introductory Exposition*

capture God in our private propositions, faith statements, or creeds. Just when we think we have grasped God, we realize he has slipped through our fingers again.

It is no surprise that today we hear much more than formerly about people being disillusioned with institutional religion, while at the same time there is everywhere evidence for an increased interest in personal spirituality of one kind or another. Religious traditions have often become so stereotyped that they no longer stir inquiring humans to vital spirituality. They tend to promote mere satisfaction with the forms and formalities of religious practices. Such a state of affairs can be deadly for the throbbing soul of hungry humans longing for spiritual illumination. Religious institutions have paid a huge price for allowing their routine practices to stultify human spirits, calcify human souls, and ossify precious human minds. It is a real question whether the institutions of the *Christian* tradition will ever again be able to revitalize successfully their appeal to the minds, souls, and spirits of humans with hungry hearts. The same must be said for the lack of profound spiritual depth and vitality in Judaism and Islam.

I have stated or implied repeatedly throughout this volume that its chapters are intended to promote authentic theology, in that sense, truth about God. I mean that this volume urges us to take an outlook on the essential ideas in the Bible, as well as they can be analyzed and summarized, that fosters spiritual growth along the lines Jesus and Paul proposed for us.[2] I have tried here to cut through our religious prejudices, traditions, and mistaken doctrines. I hoped to break up our emotional attachment to familiar ways of saying religious things. It encourages instead an open quest for the truth about God and what we can count on from God. We have a right to believe that our understandings about God are the truth,

---

(Philadelphia: Westminster, 1976). See also Cobb, *Process Theology as Political Theology* (Philadelphia: Westminster, 1982); David Tracy and Cobb, *Talking about God, Doing Theology in the Context of Modern Pluralism* (New York: Seabury, 1983); Cobb, *God and the World* (Philadelphia: Westminster, 1969); Griffin and Thomas J. J. Altizer, eds., *John Cobb's Theology in Process* (Philadelphia: Westminster, 1977); Cobb and Franklin I. Gamwell, eds., *Existence and Actuality: Conversations with Charles Hartshorne* (Chicago: University of Chicago Press, 1984); and Cobb, *Becoming a Thinking Christian* (Nashville: Abingdon, 1993).

2. J. Harold Ellens, *Understanding Religious Experiences: What the Bible Says About Spirituality* (Westport, CT: Praeger, 2008). See also Ellens, *Radical Grace, How Belief in a Benevolent God Benefits Our Health*, Westport, CT: Praeger, 2007).

only if they work—if they produce healthy and productive spirituality and operationally wholesome life in relationships and in society.

This book asks us to give up those psychological defenses in our psyches or souls which we do not want disturbed by the illumination of a word from God. Radically authentic theology should express the words of the Bible in such a way that it illumines, confirms, and consoles us. The Bible should be allowed to speak to each generation of humans with fresh cadences so as to disturb every component of our self-hood and world-view that is unwilling to let the quest for God's truth be open ended and new to us every day. Only in that way can we move to the greater empowerment, healing, and illumination of a full, healthy psycho-spirituality. The job of the Bible is to comfort the afflicted and afflict the comfortable, and my book has been intended to facilitate that.

To that end, the words of good grace in these chapters are earnestly relevant. Grace is a word and concept so redemptive for human existence, yet so nearly beyond human grasp, that it requires constant revisiting to really understand it. We simply need to take it in as a central part of the way we think and are. Grace may be simply defined, I suppose, as unconditional and universal affirmation of another person exactly where that person is in his or her pilgrimage, not where he or she should be, would like to be, idealizes himself or herself to be, but just where that person is! That is how God accepts us. That is the radical nature of his grace.

I have a magnificent son who is twelve years old. When he was seven, he sat down at my typewriter and wrote a poem. He is embarrassed by its simplicity now that he has grown "so much older and wiser"; but when he is as old as I am now, he will like it again, and see how wise it is and was. It simply says, "I am Brett; not Jet, not Sett, not Fret; just Brett." He does not yet realize how full of grace that self-affirmation and self-acceptance is. I hope fervently and pray without ceasing that he can hang on to that. To know and accept ourselves just where we are, realizing that it is precisely there in our journey that God affirms us and accepts us in his incomparable forgiveness and celebration, is the single most central word of the Bible. That unmerited goodwill is grace! Finding it, knowing it, embracing it within, is worth a lifetime of labor on the meanings, messages, and myths of the Bible and our historic heritage of faith.

THE BIBLICAL METAPHOR AND MESSAGE

In the dark dank dawn of a misty morning in April of 1963, the steel grey hull of a U.S. Navy ship loosed its moorings from the pier at Groton, Connecticut, drew silently out of the harbor, and cut its way keenly into the choppy waves of the north Atlantic. It was a gallant new ship and it had 167 fine red-blooded young American men on board. It's name was the USS Thresher, the navy's first atomic submarine. This was its maiden voyage, its shakedown cruise.

The Thresher made its rendezvous that morning with the mother ship at the appointed time, somewhere in the vastness of the north Atlantic. It began immediately with the prescribed sea trials, Identification of Friend and Foe, target acquisition and elimination, depth soundings, silent pursuits, communications drills, mock missile launches, and various battle tactics. At 2:14 that afternoon the real test came: a fast deep dive, secured in radio silence, to a still classified depth more than 2,000 feet below the rolling waves.

This gallant ship was equipped with the most sophisticated technology in the world. Her superb ships-company was made up of well trained men and they were excited about what they were doing. All went very well for nearly an hour as that fine ship and her 167 men drove steeply toward the bottom of the sea. Then suddenly at 3:13 the airways crackled with a desperate call, apparently from the Thresher: an SOS from a radioman, sent in high volume, but broken off suddenly in the middle.

Then there was silence!

The mother ship activated all her powerful communications machinery to reestablish contact with the Thresher; but there was only silence. Silence all that afternoon—as the mother ship notified Naval Headquarters in Groton, Washington, and Norfolk. Silence all that night as the U.S. Navy flexed her mighty muscles round the world in a desperate effort to rescue the Thresher and her men. But the silence continued all the next day, as deep submersibles were brought to the site from Woods Hole, Massachusetts.

Utter silence all that week!

Silence to all eternity!

That gallant ship and her 167 men were sunk in the depths of the sea. Lost! Gone! Erased as though they had never been! What is sunk in the depths of the sea cannot be recovered; cannot again be raised up, cannot be resurrected; cannot be brought back, for good or ill. What is lost in the depths of the sea is erased.

The Prophet Micah declared that God has cast all our sins into the depths of the sea. These are his surprising ancient words.

> Who is a God like our God?
> He pardons iniquity.
> He passes over transgression.
> He does not keep his anger forever.
> He delights in steadfast love.
> He is faithful to us when we are unfaithful to him.
> He tramples all our iniquities under his feet.
> He casts all our sins into the depths of the sea.
> (Micah 7:18–20)

God has cast all our sins into the depths of the sea. Lost, gone, erased; *never* to be recovered. They cannot be resurrected against us again: all our sins, short comings, dysfunctions, and inadvertent unkindness and thoughtlessness, are gone as though they had never been. They do not count anymore, and can never count against us. So Jeremiah can say with confidence, "God injects a new covenant—hence, a new consciousness into our hearts; a new law God writes there that says 'They are my people in spite of themselves. That is the law.'" Who is a God like our God?

The prophet Micah lived long before the Gospel of John was written. In that gospel we have those interesting lines that say that the old law came through Moses, but this grace and truth came through Jesus Christ. Micah lived at times of enormous turbulence and moral tragedy in Israel. In Micah's day the manipulative power-and-wealth oligarchy in Israel would sell the poor for a pair of shoes. If this sounds like twentieth-century Enron or the greedy Wall Street-induced crash of twenty-first-century America, it almost certainly is!

Egregious monsters, ruined trillions of dollars of middle-class livelihood, while collecting obscenely monstrous bonuses for having done nothing significant except destroy our carefully and diligently crafted world! Micah, the prophet said that the smoke of ancient Israelite piety and religious ceremonies was a stench in the nostrils of the Almighty. God apparently also thinks those kind of Wall-Street crimes, ancient or modern, are obscene. Micah saw his moment in time as a wretched season of a covenant-breaking and God-forsaking culture. Sounds familiar!

Micah knew that if he were to cause a real change in Israel he needed to change humans at the heart. To do that he needed to find the most memorable metaphor he could craft, that would stick in their psycho-spiritual gullets, so they could not puke it out. He knew he had to free them from their fear, guilt, and shame; so they could spend their psycho-spiritual energies on growing toward God. Therefore, he picked this unforgettable image. God has cast all our sins into the depths of the sea. The Book of Revelation calls it the sea of God's eternal forgetfulness.

Other metaphors would not work. Micah's knew that God does not shoot our sins into outer space in hermetically sealed capsules. Even Micah knew already in the mid-700s BCE that what goes up must come down. Remember Apollo 13. Micah did not picture God burying our sins in the sands of the seashore at ebb tide. He knew even then what children learn with fascination in each new generation. What always happens to hidden pirates chests on mysterious islands in children's books? They are eventually discovered, washed up on shore; and brought into court as evidence against the wretched evildoer.

Only *this* specific, memorable metaphor that Micah chose could do the work well enough and permanently enough to tell God's real story. God has cast all our sins into the depths of the sea. Gone, lost forever, erased as never having been at all. They are never recoverable. They can never again be resurrected against us! Does that sound OK for those Wall-street bastards? Of course not! But it is as true for them as it is for us! Micah said that is simply how God works. He is not in the business of shaping us up, but in the work of saving us completely from ourselves, in the long run. All of us! God is that radical, unconditional, and universal in his grace.

So that is Micah's memorable metaphor and Jeremiah's radical concept of covenant. What, then, is the message here? Why, of course, that with God to forgive is to forget. God looks at you and me, indeed, at all humanity, and God cannot remember that we are sinners, inadequate and flawed humans, who continue to fall short of the mark; who in Paul's words always come short of the glorious destiny God has designed for us, since we are made in God's own image.

The memorable message of Micah is the same as Jesus' message in the Parable of the Prodigal Son. Of course this parable should really be known as the Parable of the Waiting Father, as the great German preacher, Helmut Thielicke,[3] used to say. It is, after all, a story about the surprising nature of the father, not the rather common reprehensible behavior of the prodigal son. It turns out that the issue at stake in that parable is never the question of the father's unconditional acceptance of the sons. The issue at stake is always the question of the sons' capacity for unconditional acceptance of the father's unconditional acceptance. This is the case for both the prodigal son, and for his elder brother as well. The sons represent us. The father is the God-figure in the parable, of course.

That is our human predicament today—as it was for ancient Israel. So Micah's marvelously memorable metaphor brings precisely the meaningful message Jesus wanted to nail down, once and for all. What is that crucial meaning? We cannot sin ourselves out of God's grace. We cannot squirm out of God's long embrace. Nobody can! Ever! Forever! God's grace is that radical, and that unconditional, and that universal.

So the reason to be God's people is not to save our bloody souls from hell. The only reason to be a Christian is because it is more fun. More fun to live all of life, through all its ups and downs, in the full assurance of God's grace. Being a Christian is not a command, but an invitation; not an obligation but an opportunity, not a burden to be labored under and sweated out for a lifetime, but a possibility to be seized and celebrated, now and forevermore.

Most of us do not want such radical grace. I do not want such radical grace. If grace is that radical and God's acceptance and forgiveness of me is that unconditional, then I must give up the conditionality of my relationship with you, regardless of your character, quality, race, creed, or gender. I must embrace you in spite of yourself, and open myself to such an equal embrace.

Moreover, I do not like such radical grace for another reason. It means I have no ultimate control over my ultimate destiny, over my relationship with God. I cannot be an illustrious churchman for sixty years and secretly think in my heart that it gives me some extra leverage with God. I cannot live my life all week in charity and grace and then on Saturday night grab God by the shirt collar and declare, "God, you owe me!" Like the prodigal son, I cannot even sign up to do God's will and work as God's *servant*. God insists that to God I am his son—in spite

---

3. Helmut Thielicke, *The Waiting Father: Sermons on the Parables of Jesus*, trans. John W. Doberstein (New York: Harper & Row, 1959).

of myself; and so is every human in the perplexing journey of life. My option is then to decide to behave like God's person.

Notice that remarkable moment when the prodigal son returns home! His father has been waiting long days and weeks, months and years for his sons return. Every morning he has looked down that long dusty road with no avail and little hope. Silently he has waited to see his lost son. Meanwhile his son wasted his treasure, dissipated his health, degraded his life, until he finally landed at the very bottom rung of society. He has sunk in desperation to the menial task of herding pigs. A rich Jewish boy, herding pigs just to keep himself from starving!

In that sad state the prodigal son finally came to himself. Pain has a way of driving us into ourselves and starting the engine of growth and healing. He remembered that his father's servants lived in luxury; and there he lay starving in the filthy mire of the pig pen. Then and there he resolved to get up, go home, confront his father, and negotiate for a position as a servant in his father's house. He kept his promise to himself. All his other options had been exhausted. From his filthy dissipation he simply had to go home and come clean. So he went to see his father.

Now that patient, waiting father, of course, saw the son coming down the road before the son saw him. His father ran to him, threw his arms around the boy and embraced him; but you can almost see the son pushing the father away as he declares, "Wait a minute, father. You do not understand my situation. I am no longer worthy to be called your son. I have wasted my life, lost my inheritance, defiled the family name, and degraded my self completely. I am not worthy to be called your son. Instead, hire me as one of your servants. This much I have learned. My only chance is to be embraced in your wholesome household. Hire me so I can prove by diligence and responsibility to be worthy of your esteem and honor once again."

If you read a bit between the lines you can see the heartbeat of this silent waiting father. He declares to the son, in effect, "You want me to make you my hired man? Hired man, indeed! You cannot ever be my hired man. You are my son. You will always be my son. Oh, I realize that you do not look like my son anymore, you probably do not feel like my son, you are not thinking like my son, you do not talk like my son, you do not reason like my son, you have not behaved like a son of mine, and after all that time in the pig pen, you surely do not smell like my son—but you are my son."

"You are my son because I am your father. You will be my son as long as I chose to father you. You are not my son because of the quality of your character and behavior. You are my son because of the quality of my character and behavior as your father. You will be my son as long as I faithfully father you, and I will never give you up. You are my son in spite of yourself, because I am so much your father in my heart that I cannot help myself. You want to be my hired man so you can prove to me that deep down inside you really are a good guy. You are having trouble accepting unconditionally my unconditional acceptance of you. But when you have a son you will know that it is precisely in that the real fathering is centered."

The prodigal son is like all of us. He wants that power in the equation of relationship with the father that depends upon his ability to prove himself worthy, instead of simply accepting his inherent worthiness, as son. The father, however, insists, "You are not my son because of your character or behavior but because of my character and behavior as your father."

So then they threw a big feast to celebrate the return of the lost son.

Now, the prodigal son's elder brother would not come to the feast and celebrate. He was the son who had always done the right and responsible thing. He was a good guy and he could not stand all the fuss about his rotten brother who had now finally dragged himself back home in desperation. When the father noticed the elder brother's absence he went out on the farm to find out why. He sat down with his elder son and again invited him to the celebration. In a fury the elder brother spit out through his clenched teeth, "All these years I have done my duty and you never celebrated me. Now this wasteful scoundrel returns home destitute, and you act like this is the Second Coming."

Well, that sounds like good reasoning, does it not? All those long years of the prodigal son's dilatory absence, the elder brother had carefully tended the farm, protected the estate, managed the investments, and cared for the elderly parents. He had been a good churchman for all those twenty-five years, obedient, respectful, predictable, and responsible. Why had the father not adequately celebrated him?

To this the father replies in effect, "Son, all that I possess belongs to you. Your brother has taken his share. You inherit the farm and all the estate. Surely you know that is my expression to you of gratitude for all you do. However, if you think I love you because of all your faithfulness and obedience as a good son or a good churchman all these years, your problem is the same as your brother's. I do not love and celebrate you because of your faithful obedience. I love you because I am your father. You are not my son because of the quality of your character and behavior. You are my beloved son because of my character and behavior. I love you as my son because I am your father. You will be my beloved son as long as I insist on faithfully fathering you, and I will never give you up.

"If you were a responsible person and a diligent son just to make sure I loved you, you should have raised more hell. You should have taken more freedom. You should have had more fun. You cannot sin yourself out of my grace nor squirm out of my long embrace. You are too worried about appearances and prescriptions. You are ticked off because we are celebrating your rotten brother's return.

"Do you not see that he was dead to me and he is alive again? He was lost to me and he is found! *Nothing else counts*! It is appropriate for us to celebrate."

So radical is God's grace, so unconditional—and so absolutely universal! There will be no human left behind. That is the main stream of the Bible's main theme, and through that we must read the creeds, fashion our faith, and critique the long story of every religious tradition. So it is worth repeating Micah's signal words:

> Who is a God like our God?
> He pardons iniquity.
> He passes over transgression.
> He does not keep his anger forever.
> He delights in steadfast love.
> He is faithful to us when we are unfaithful to him.
> He tramples all our iniquities under his feet.
> He casts all our sins into the depths of the sea.
> And he guaranteed this to us before we were conceived,
> Promised it to us through our ancestors in the days of old.
> (Micah 7:18–20)

17

The Chemistry of Forgiveness

WELL, IF THAT IS what God is like, it strongly suggests what humans, made in God's image, might be expected to be like. In chapters fourteen and fifteen I dealt with the tragic consequences that sicken human life and thought when we project sick notions upon God, turning him into a monster. However, if our understanding of God is a notion of a healthy God, surely we will automatically become similarly healthy persons. At least such a theological or biblical perception of God's nature and behavior as the one Micah knew, will inspire healthy people to be unconditional, radical, and universal in our inclination to make forgiveness the mainstay of our lifestyle. We will want to be forgiving people, it seems to me. In chapter 8 I dealt only briefly with the theme of the forgiveness of sins because I wished to deal with it here with adequately extensive treatment. That is warranted by the universal fact of life that people who truly understand the divine intimations and illuminations in the Bible develop a genuine expectation that the mainstay of a wholesome life is forgiveness.

The difficulty with this expectation, of course, is that forgiveness requires great risks and is often very costly. What if the person you forgive just uses your forgiveness as license to continue to abuse you in some way? What if that person simply does not grasp the meaning of being forgiven, or does not care to be forgiven? Of course, it is not as though God does not wrestle with these same enigmatic questions. That is the amazing thing about grace. It does seriously take up all those questions, and then sets them all aside as having far less priority than forgiveness. So grace just goes and does it, as a pre-condition to everything else.

Think of the main metaphor, for example, that we get from Jesus life. One day he stopped thinking about, fooling with, and worrying the attitude of the religious authorities who were out to get him. That day he just decided to go and do the deed. The gospel says that he set his face steadfastly to go to Jerusalem and face the consequences of his promotion of God's radical forgiveness of friends and enemies. He marched straight to the cross, as we know. Hanging there on that Roman cross on that black Friday, he prayed for the men who crucified him. He said, "Father, forgive them. They do not know what it really is that they are doing."

The message of Good Friday can be boiled down to this: forgiveness is worth dying for. The message of Easter is just as simple and profound: forgiveness is worth living for. Forgiveness is worth putting one's life on the line for. Until that first Good Friday the ethic in the human community everywhere was the law of tooth and claw. That jungle code was "an eye for an eye and a tooth for a tooth." Jesus said, instead, "Love your enemy, and pray for those that spitefully use you."

The new thing that began at the cross on Good Friday, and set forgiveness at the center of all of God's operations in this world, was the message that forgiveness is worth dying for and worth living for. Can you imagine how things in this world would change if Jesus' message could be insinuated into the minds and hearts of all the conflicting adversaries in the world today. What a radical change would happen, if that even got a real good start with you and me personally. What if that divine spirit got loose in the world?

Simon Wiesenthal was a Jew who lived in Vienna. He spent his life, from 1945 on, tracking down Nazis and bringing them to justice whenever possible—the criminal politicians who were powerful and popular in the European world during the time of Adolf Hitler. Simon Wiesenthal did not always sit comfortably with his chosen occupation. He told a story about one of his real life situations in his book *The Sunflowers*. If you get a chance to read it you will want to do so. It is a small book that you can read quickly in a Sunday afternoon. It will change your life.

In that little book Wiesenthal tells the real life story of his having been taken, as a German Jew, and impressed into a work party by the Gestapo during World War II. His work party was sent to a military hospital that received the more serious casualties from the eastern front. He was assigned as the leader of a maintenance group responsible for the care of the grounds of the facility. One day he was called by a ward orderly to see a young man who was begging for someone like Wiesenthal. The young man was twenty-two. He had been conscripted into the German army at age eighteen and impressed into the SS troops. The SS perpetrated the worst war crimes during the Hitler-era.

The young lad had been assigned to the extermination of a Jewish ghetto somewhere in eastern Europe. Subsequently he had been injured in an explosion, blinded by it, and hospitalized in serious condition. He was the son of a Lutheran pastor, but during his military years he had replaced his faith tradition with the ideology of the Nazis. Now he lay near death and wanted to confess to some significant Jewish person how he and his fellow soldiers had set fire to the Jewish tenements and had shot the women and children as they jumped from the windows and tried to escape that holocaust.

Wiesenthal went to see the young man and sat at his bed for two hours while the soldier poured out his heart. Wiesenthal said nothing except that he would return the next day, which he did. He sat there for a number of hours again and the man implored his forgiveness, having come back to the passions and perceptions of his earlier religious life. Wiesenthal came back the third day and sat for about an hour. By that point, he says, he was so thoroughly overwhelmed and disgusted with the entire thing that, without letting the blind lad know, he got up and silently left.

Wiesenthal struggled to such an extent with his unforgiving act that it gave him nightmares. Finally he wrote the story and sent it to a number of philosophers and theologians who deal with issues of ethics, in the Jewish, Catholic, and Protestant communities. He asked them what he should have done. "Should I, could I, have forgiven that young man for those reprehensible things?"

Many Jewish scholars wrote back and said, "You couldn't forgive him. Nobody can forgive him except the people that he slaughtered." Others said, "You can't forgive him, only God can forgive him." Some said they would never forgive him. Indeed, they would have strangled him there in his bed.

A famous Roman Catholic theologian, Jacques Maritain, said, "Simon, you should have forgiven him. He made his confession to you. You were God's man on the spot. God forgives him. You should have forgiven him, in the name of God and on his behalf." The most impressive response, it seems to me, came from Martin Marty, a Lutheran historian and theologian from the University of Chicago. He said, "Simon, Jacques Maritain is correct. You should have forgiven him. God forgives him.

He was making his confession to you and you were God's agent there. You should have forgiven him. But there are other reasons you should have forgiven him. First of all, you are getting way too much mileage out of your guilt. Secondly, forgiveness frees the forgiver more than the forgiven."

Jesus understood clearly that the psycho-spiritual impact of the act of forgiving is indeed the channel and the agency of the Divine Spirit that changes human being's lives. That is why in our previous chapter Micah made it so plain that our calling is nothing more and nothing less than the kind of unconditional forgiveness with which God handles us. Wiesenthal should have forgiven the pathetic Lutheran lad because that would have freed Simon Wiesenthal from carrying around all his life the burden of guilt, perplexity, and shame that compelled him to write *Sunflowers* and send it around the world. Reading that book we immediately discern that its author struggles with the anguish that he did wrong in failing to forgive. The cancer of it was stuck in his heart and he could not puke it out. The boy was free in God's forgiveness and eternity. Simon Wiesenthal could not get free of it. He died with that burden torturing his heart.

On February 15, 1993, *Time* magazine had an interesting article called "The Chemistry of Love," from which I have adapted the title of this chapter. That article was significant in that it claimed that love and forgiveness are basically just a matter of biochemistry. It said that most of us know the exciting feeling that we experience when we suddenly seem to connect with another person in that exotic way we call falling in love. *Time* magazine, on the basis of some very extensive biochemical research, said it is just chemistry.

What happens is that certain kinds of triggers that our brains recognize are set off by some other person's appearance, behavior, or style; and when that happens that cranks up our endocrine system to produce four chemicals that have the same effect as amphetamines. We often refer to it in popular expressions as "the chemistry, or the electricity, of falling in love." When we fall in love we go into what feels like some kind of altered state. We distinguish this kind of "being in love," from the more ordinary experience of loving someone in care and kindness.

"I have fallen in love! It is not just that I love him, I am *in love with him.*" Four amphetamines do the job. According to the article these seem to last about four years and then our bodies run out of the capacity to keep on pumping those amphetamines. After that follows the onset of a different kind of chemistry. It is a flood of oxytocin through our blood stream, and that has the net effect of giving us the feeling of devotion, endurance, commitment, and sustaining interest and passion.

Well, I am sure that there is some truth to that. I vow never to give up on the notion that there is something more than chemistry, something exotic and spiritual, about falling in love. I hope it lasts forever for you and me. In any case, being in love, or just loving another human in care and kindness, surely is the context of true forgiveness. God forgives us in spite of ourselves; and the real work of loving another person is to love and forgive that person in spite of himself or herself. Anybody can love someone who is perfect. The divine call is to love and forgive those who are not, and to be able to receive that kind of love and forgiveness ourselves. Jesus said, "Even the pagans love their friends. The unique thing about godliness is to love your enemies and do good to those who despitefully use you."

It is interesting that Jesus' entire approach to this business of forgiveness was not concern about some theoretical principle of or approach to forgiveness. It was not some theory or theology about God's equation of forgiveness and where we fit in. Jesus was not preoccupied with *how* we are called to forgiveness and that sort of thing. Jesus' approach was always pragmatic and operational. If you forgive people their sins now, he said to his disciples, they will be forgiven for all eternity and if you do not forgive them, then they are locked in, they are in bondage until you forgive them, and so are you. His was an operational and practical concern!

I suspect that what Jesus understood to be behind that imperative was something like the science behind the article in *Time* magazine. To be genuinely forgiving means to transcend all of our feelings of defensiveness, rage, grief, and hurt. It means being able to step over that injury that cannot be rationalized away, cannot be understood, or is completely unexplainable. Such unaccountable evil can only be disposed of by forgiving it. Otherwise we are stuck with carrying it around in our hearts as a burden for the rest of our lives. Jesus understood that when we take that action of stepping over that injury, we set in motion a lot of forces inside ourselves. These may actually include our biochemistry. These forces shift our sense of things, our mindset, and our attitudes toward relationship and healing.

I run into people all of the time in my clinical work who are caught in their incapacity to forgive a serious relational injury. The net effect is that the person who did the injury probably does not even know about it. The person who has been injured, because he or she cannot forgive, is destined for a whole life long, to carry that cancer in the soul. Forgiveness frees the forgiver psycho-spiritually, and who knows, maybe even psycho-biologically. That was the brand new idea that exploded upon the world at the cross of Christ. He said of those who were pounding the nails through his hands, "Father, forgive them for they know not what they do," and *that* profound life changing truth got loose in the world. It is the passion of the divine spirit in human hearts and minds to this day.

Many churches have been noted throughout history for their sophisticated theology and well worked out world and life view. That has at some times pushed us into intellectualizing the gospel, rather than internalizing it. Jesus would not have tolerated that kind of spirituality. One day Jesus and his disciples, Peter, James, and John, were picnicking on a mountain when they saw a vision that seemed to come from heaven. Peter's response was, "Man, we ought to just set up shop here. This is such an exotic event. We should build here some places to stay. We could remain in this mountaintop experience a long time."

Do you know what Jesus' response was to that theoretical, escapist attitude about spirituality? He grabbed all three of them and slammed their heads together and took them down the mountain and stuck them into the face of a demon-possessed child and said, "This kind you cannot heal except by prayer and fasting. Get down to business." He took them off the spiritual mountaintop and grounded them in the mud, sand, and slime of human suffering on this earth. That is practical, operational stuff!

If you forgive people their sins they will be forgiven. You will set in motion in them a chemistry of the spirit that will change their lives and heal them from those things for which there is no other kind of healing. I had a really good friend, Lewis Smedes, who spent most of his academic life at Fuller Seminary School of Theology. He wrote a book entitled, *Forgive and Forget*. It is a good book. Not a great book, but there is one great statement in it. He said we should all forgive unconditionally, as God does, but we should not forgive and forget, as God does. We should forgive and remember. We should remember what we have forgiven and leave it forgiven. We should remember that it was forgiven and never resurrect it, as we typically do in moments of passion or dysfunction.

It is amazing to me how readily humans can take back the forgiveness they claim they give to one another. This is particularly true between husbands and wives. They come to my clinic and after a good amount of therapy they can sometimes get to the point at which they both wish to forgive whatever it was that troubled their relationship. One would think that would settle a lot of misery. But they come back some time later and their new story is that something came up between them, or one of them got some kind of chemistry shift, and out came all the original anger as though nothing had been forgiven. We all know that if you want to pick a fight, any excuse is a good enough excuse. Then in the middle of the bitching and moaning, everything from the last thirty years get dragged up again. Did they not really forgive it back then? Of course they did at that time. But they forgot that they forgave it? With God, as Micah said, to forgive is to forget. Smedes says that with us to forgive includes remembering that we forgave.

Nothing heals anything like forgiveness heals. We should remember to celebrate what has been forgiven. Keep the savor of the flavor of that experience alive in ourselves and in the forgiven ones. We should rejoice about it and take courage in it all life long. If you and I do not cultivate the experience of forgiving how will we recognize the experience when we see God face to face—where, according to Micah, there is nothing but forgiveness? "I believe in the Holy Spirit . . . the forgiveness of sins!" Yeah, right on!

PART FOUR

Summary and Conclusion

18

A Godly Way of Life

IN THIS SUMMARY AND conclusion to all we have explored in this book, I should like to recap some of the key ideas and memorable illustrations that I have woven into the first seventeen chapters. I hope in this way to install the main metaphors, narratives, and arguments permanently in your minds so that those ideas may be nailed down in your memory and stimulate richer spiritual life for anyone who seriously works through this volume.

It is quite interesting, I think, that the idea of such radical forgiveness, as that which I discussed in chapter 17, seems most of the time to be counter-intuitive. It just does not normally look like the thing that is going to work best. Most humans are in the habit of assuming that life is a *quid-pro-quo* game, that is, life is about settling scores. Even in all the talk, both secular and religious, that people do about justice, it generally sounds to me like a justification for avoiding forgiveness and unconditional grace in the way we deal with each other. In our day and age, with all its talk about equality and justice, both of these notions have been turned into ethical idols and political weapons of propaganda.

Justice is not so important as mercy and grace. God is merciful and *just* to forgive us our sins, the Bible declares. The only justice from God's point of view is mercy and forgiving grace, for the likes of us. Do you know what is just in this world? It is the kind of forgiving mercy and grace that resolves the problem, and does not just settle the score or pay evil for evil, or even guarantee equal opportunity. In the evil for evil equation, the cost-benefit analysis never comes out in anybody's benefit. In the good for evil equation the cost-benefit balance always comes out good for everyone's benefit.

I think it is a comic tragedy that so much religion throughout history has been dominated so much of the time by a great variety of heresies.

A heresy is a false teaching. We are all heretics and we all ought to settle with that up front; because it is a very important part of our pilgrimage in life to realize that we are often coming at the issues of God's truth, and our own perceptions of truth, from a false beginning point. We are usually tempted to perceive and formulate our faith in notions about God, about ourselves, about the world, salvation, and eternal hope that are incomplete ideas at best.

Certainly our insights are always in some way distorted from what reality must look like from God's perspective. To the extent that our notions are incomplete and distorted, they are false. We must, of course, live with the truth that we perceive, but always remember at the same time that we do not know ultimate truth. Our best perceptions are only approximations of what God knows to be the truth. So our truth, even if it works fairly well for us, is actually a heresy. We might as well look at that state of affairs with humor since we cannot ever completely fix this problem.

Most humans tend to be very dogmatic about what they believe, as though they really have captured God or truth in their theological propositions. Religious institutions of every kind have acted like they have God under control in the formulations of their creeds and traditions. That has never been true, of course, and it is an arrogant heresy to suppose so. This book is designed to expose some of those heresies and offer some better alternatives. However, even the proposals, cautions, and corrections this book offers are not God's ultimate truth. We are all merely pilgrims in a quest for glimmers of understanding, and we are always more blind than sighted, because we are human. Our best perceptions of God's truth are human perceptions from this human and earthly side of the equation. Human insights are always limited by our limited human capacity to understand and by the earth-bound level of our information and outlook.

The Christian churches have tended to act all through the centuries as though we had available to us, and under our control, God's ultimate truth. The fact is that we have never been able to closely approximate God's truth, as far as we can tell, and only God knows what the ultimate, absolute truth is. Moreover, God is very subtle. He reveals himself to us only by intimations, not by plainly spoken theological treatises or specific detailed definitions. Therefore, my claim is that everybody inevitably falls into heresy; that is, into perceiving the truth about God falsely, distorted, and incomplete at best.

The real problem with that is not that there is something fundamentally wrong with our being simply human. The real problem with that is that being human and limited to human perceptions of the truth about God always puts us in the dangerous position of cutting the taproot of God's real grace to us. That will always cut off the very source of our healthy spirituality. Because as soon as we formulate what seems, inside of our hearts or minds, to be a really good statement about what we feel or understand about God, we have already formulated a human concept. It is always, as I said, incomplete and, hence, to some degree a heresy. Now if we act or feel that humanely fashioned faith is absolute truth, we are immediately boxing ourselves into a limiting capsule of mere human insight. We are, therefore, fencing ourselves out of God's own grand perspective on what really is. It may be the best we can do, but it is a heresy. The best we can do, therefore, is to keep the truth-quest open-ended.

Let me illustrate this with a brief review of the most important aspect of the parable of the prodigal son that I discussed in more detail in a previous chapter. In that wonderful story, the prodigal son eventually decides that he has really blown it with his life. He realizes that it is profoundly ridiculous that he is starving in a pig pen while his father's servants are living in luxury. He realizes his life is a really bad joke! Soon, driven by this desperation and real starvation, the son thinks up a solution: He says to himself, "I will go to my father and I will say to my father, 'I have sinned in the sight of heaven and before your sight.'" So he gets up and goes home.

When the prodigal son arrives home, he offers his father a deal. The young man seems to have been really changed. He has turned his life around. He has been converted from a runaway wastrel to a thoughtful fellow, oriented upon his father's home and value system. The difficulty is that the son has been converted straight into a heresy. The deal he offers his father is that he be taken back as the hired man, so he can prove that deep down inside he really is a good guy, despite his wretched arrogant life. He wants to justify himself, rather than simply accept his abject neediness and throw himself into his father's unconditional forgiveness and acceptance of him, thus freeing him for a good future.

The son's need to justify himself is the heresy. This son has really done everything wrong. He thinks the solution is to work his way back into his father's favor. He thinks the solution is to be given a chance for self-justification. He wants to keep his own hands on the controls and not be abjectly indebted to his father's grace and love. The difficulty is that he could work for the next thirty years and do well, but it would not take away the fact that he wasted a million dollars and the best years of his life, as well as putting his father through all those years of grief and alienation.

Self-justification does not fix the original problem. Self-righteousness and self-justification do not change the tragic history of that past. He thinks they do. "Let me prove myself to you. Hire me as a servant and I will prove to you by being a diligent, responsible person, that despite my external behavior all these years, way down deep inside I really am OK. That's the real me."

That is a heresy in the sense that it is a false view of reality. The reality is that he is the son. He is a rotten son, now in utter disrepute, but he is the son. That is what he must face up to. The issue is not about his facing up to twenty years of hard work to prove himself. Of course, that is taken for granted one way or the other. The issue is to face himself as the son whose situation can only be healed by a father's forgiveness.

The father's response, of course, to that plea for self-righteousness and self-justification, is definitive and radical. "How can you be my servant? You are my son. That does not depend on your behavior. It depends on my behavior as your father, and you cannot sin yourself out of my love."

His father assures him that everything in the end is of grace: unconditional forgiveness and acceptance. Nothing else fixes all the wasted years, lost treasure, and alienated relationship. Nothing can justify that. Nothing can rationalize it. Nothing can make it understandable or excusable. The only thing that fixes it is forgiveness and unconditional love. Forgiveness is what we do for those horrid things than cannot be explained. Thus by forgiveness, sin, fear, guilt, and shame are eliminated from God's equation. They are not only discounted. They are erased. They do not count now or ever. They will never count against us. Why is it so difficult for us to swallow that truth of God? In recent years the sunken Titanic has been relocated, but in the end it must be left there at the bottom of the sea, where God has cast our sins.

There are five heresies that we regularly fall into, any one of which can be spiritually defeating. They have been implied obliquely in all the chapters of this entire book. Let me summarize them here and state them concretely. The first one is the one I just described: substituting conditional grace for God's unconditional grace. This is the very common notion: that God forgives, accepts, cherishes, and saves us because we please him or because we confess our sins. You cannot imagine how many people I meet who really believe the heresy that God forgives humans because we turn out in the end to be good people, or because we beg him for salvation, or go to confession, or attend church, or contribute to charity. That almost universally reigning idea is a heresy. God does not accept, forgive, love, and save us because of the way we posture ourselves. God is gracious because God is grace. God's grace exudes from him in such a constituent way that it is his nature. He cannot help himself. God cannot be anything but grace, in spite of our nature or behavior. Anything else would be untrue to God's inherent nature. If God were not a God of such a radical kind of grace, God would be a heretic.

The second heresy that we tend to fall into, and that can really ruin healthy spirituality, is the notion that substitutes sentimentality for real Christian love. That is not of the Divine Spirit. Such a notion substitutes mere sympathy for true empathy, as though Christian love means something "nice and sweet." That is too superficial. Sentimentality is a kind of self-indulgence, not in keeping with the nature of the Holy Spirit in the world and in our lives. It's not real love for that other person. In a sense it is the opposite of the tough stuff that Christian love really is. True Christian love is willing to intervene and renovate things if that is what is necessary to the advantage and healing of the person being helped, regardless whether that person knows it or likes it.

Christian love moves us to invest ourselves arbitrarily in what that person needs, not what that person wants. In the end we have no choice but to "play God", because who is to decide what the other person needs? We are human, so we must use our best judgment, go for it, and love that person by acting in ways that really change things for him or her, if they cannot or will not do so themselves. Change what needs to be changed in that person's life insofar as we have the ability and responsibility to affect it.

I was a soldier for many years of my life. I have a young friend who is just back from the Iraq War. He experienced the trauma of combat in which he served as a skillful infantry medic. Now he is in college, but he is medicating his traumatic memories with large doses of alcohol. He gets drunk every night to get himself to sleep. He likes to stay at my home on the night before he has an early morning class because I live across from the school and he lives forty miles away. I am glad to have him and he likes the camaraderie of our shared military experience. He knows I understand and love him.

However, how should I love him? Well, I will not get drunk with him though he would like me to do so. Sometimes when he is drunk he acts like he wishes me to make love with him. That is not my taste or orientation, and I do not think it is his either when he is sober. He is a lonely lost soul, as you can see. How does one love such a guy?

Well, I decided to try to provide him what he needs not what he wants. I told him he could not come to my house drunk or on drugs, nor drink at my house, and he had to go to a physician I recommended and get medication to assist his sleep. I had to actually take him to the physician and pay for the appointment, but the doctor treated him, put him on a regimen, and gave him medication for depression and for sleep. The medication works well as long as he takes it. He came to my home sober and enjoyed being healthier, clear headed, and focused for the first time in a long time. Sometimes he likes to lose himself in drunkenness more than he likes feeling healthy, and then we have to start over.

Love, real Christian love, is surgical: willing to turn the loved person inside out and upside down if that is required for his or her healing. Most of us know that a family intervention is the only thing that works with most addicts of any kind. That intervention is tough love: the embodiment of love and forgiveness. I will either succeed in loving this young man with the interventions of tough love or he will die young. Christian love is not just nice and sweet sympathy. It is in this way that I am called to be the channel of the Divine Spirit in this young soldier's life.

The third heresy that we tend to fall into is the notion that God has total power in this world, and is, therefore, totally responsible for things. There are people who really believe that it is God's will when a little boy is killed by a tractor, or a volcano kills Columbians or Italians. The truth is that God is not in control of those things. God has created this world, set it in motion, and given it to us. The Bible has made it plain to us: "You be fruitful and multiply and replenish the earth and you have dominion over it" (Genesis 1:28).

If we do not act on behalf of Columbians who are sufficiently uninformed that they want to live at the side of a mountain vulnerable to mudslides, God cannot save them. If we do not act on behalf of the citizens of Pompey who live next to Mt. Vesuvius, which every thousand years volcanically blows its top, God cannot save the wonderful people of Pompeii and Herculaneum. If we do not act on behalf of those who are being treated unjustly in the world, God cannot act to deliver them. If we do not get Osama bin Laden, God cannot. If we did not put an end to Hitler's genocide, God could not end it. If we do not forgive the offenders, God cannot mediate his forgiveness into their lives.

If we do not stop the Hitlers, the Mussolinis, the Stalins, the Saddam Husseins, and the other arrogant, abusive dictators in this world, God cannot corral the consequences of their mayhem. If we do not stop the lethargy and partisanship of the U.S. Congress that renders it immobile instead of efficient in the work needed to keep America safe and prosperous, God cannot bless our land with wise political operations.

God takes us so seriously that he leaves it up to us. He will not violate the inherent dynamics of our personality development to solve our problems for us. God will not intervene upon the cause and effect processes in history in order to straighten things out and pay us off on Saturday night. He respects the pristine role of those dynamics. It is up to us to act in God's way.

If we do not act, God's providence cannot bless. Providence is always responsive, not initiatory. However, if we initiate the proper action of loving care, God can providentially prosper it, or withhold his prospering spirit from our undertakings if they are not the workable ones. It is a heresy to think that God is in control and to count on him to change things, hope against hope, when that is not God's business, but ours.

The fourth heresy that tends to wreak havoc on the spirituality of Christians is the notion that Christianity is an individualistic religion, in which personal piety is separate from the reformative demands of love and justice in the church and in society. Many of us have tended to be in the forefront of social action in this world, in God's name. That took a great deal of treasure and hours of hard work over the decades and centuries. That is as it should be. But in the process we made some bad choices that landed us in a kind of church-ianity instead of Christianity, in a kind of project Christianity instead of authentic and useful Christian action in the world. This usually happened when we had split off our social action from the wellsprings of personal spirituality and sound theology.

Much of the thrashing about in various kinds of social action by religious people, during the 70s and 80s of the last century, was a lot of "sound and fury signifying little or nothing." The reason for its irrelevance is that such things frequently have not come out of a profound theology or a pervasive personal spirituality, or a life embracing piety. In the life of Martin Luther King Jr., his quest for sound social change did come from his authentic inner piety, and it accomplished great things. Consequently, we have come a long way on the trajectory upon which he set us. But to suppose that authentic religion or ethical behavior can take place without being infused with genuine personal spirituality is a heresy, a false view of reality. It is not the way of the Holy Spirit.

On the other hand, living personal spirituality with no effect on the reformative needs of church and society is a sham. It, too, is a heresy. It is a trivialization of what it means to be called of God in Christ, to live by the logic of the spirit of God. Shearing off religious behavior from personal spirituality is always a false kind of life. The constant reformation of church and society needs to come from the power of profound personal faith. If personal spirituality does not produce reformation in church and society, if it does not lead to growth and renewal, it does not meet the basic rubrics of true faith. If religion or spirituality do not move us to the desire and ability to be people of forgiveness, our lives are false. "I believe in the Holy Spirit: the holy universal church, the communion of the saints, and the forgiveness of sins."

The final heresy that is pervasive in the religious world is the notion that there is such a thing as cosmic evil. This often shows up as the notion that there is an evil force in God's world which has some kind of equivalence to the force of God's presence in the world. It includes the idea that we are perpetually up against that evil force. I have discussed this at length above so will only summarize here. It is a heresy to continue to promote the notion that there is some kind of negative god out there that is fighting the kingdom of God and that the upshot is still unclear. There is no evidence for the existence of a devil, Satan, or hell. None whatsoever! "I believe in God, the father almighty, maker of heaven and earth and . . . I believe in the Holy Spirit . . ." I do not believe in a devil.

As I said, there is no empirical evidence for an evil force in the world. You and I cannot cite a single instance in all of history that would lead us to the conclusion that there is anything out there besides God, present in his creation, providence, and grace. There is no evidence for anything else in experience or in scripture, if it is properly read and understood. The notion that there were devils, the devil, or hell never entered into the biblical faith tradition until the Israelites were in exile in Babylon and got those heretical ideas from a pagan religion called Zoroastrianism. Zoroastrianism is a religion in which the notion of God and Devil, light and darkness, good and evil are equal forces arrayed against each other.

The reason that the Judahites in Babylonian exile hooked into that pagan idea, for which there was no evidence, was that they thought it explained how it was possible that God's wonderful people, the Israelites, got overrun by the Babylonians and carried off into exile. They were asking, "How is God in history." They were trying to explain an existential fact in their own history and they adopted that false, pagan notion in order to try to explain their personal predicament.

That was, of course, the cultural matrix into which Jesus was born and in terms of which he related his message. So he uses the metaphors and that language of sheep and goats, outer darkness, Gehenna, worms that never die, and the fires that are never quenched. All these metaphors were pictures of what it feels like in life when we are separated from authentic spirituality, from communion with the saints, and from God.

Jesus was so human that he was conditioned by his humanness and his cultural setting and ideas. He had to speak in the language and metaphors of his moment if he was to speak at all. He himself makes that fact plain to us at a number of places in the gospels. Even so, he seldom uses such language or metaphors.

But to suppose that evil is a supernatural force out there is to skew the entire quest of Christians before the face of God. There is nothing out there except God. Evil does not exist in this world except in the nasty things we do to each other. Even if we seem to be trying to speak against evil, we are using an idolatrous idea, a heresy, to idolize evil as though it is something out there approximately as great and transcendent as God.

The *Left Behind* series of religious books are popular, I am told. They all reflect these pagan ideas and seem to give us a packaged solution of how to look at the world. I am amazed how evangelical and fundamentalist Christians and many other folk have gone after these awful narratives. They do not reflect a Christian perspective. It is a pagan perspective they promote; and if you adopt that perspective it fundamentally corrupts the possibility that you can see the world in terms of God's viewpoint. God's worldview is the perspective of unconditional and saving grace for all humankind. Tim LaHaye's gospel is Zoroastrian paganism and it is important that Christians recognize it for the heresy that it is.

There are two sides to this life, of course. That was the tragic side: we are all heretics. We are all humanly limited. Only God knows the whole story. The other side is the comic side. The comic side of our perpetual temptation to fall into these five heresies is the fact that God is not a heretic. God cherishes us. God saves us, unconditionally, forgivingly, and permanently, in spite of our humanness. In spite of our heresies! In spite of our limitations! In spite of our confusion! In spite of our wrongheadedness! The comic side is that God is not a heretic because God is God, and grace is grace, and in the end that means all is forgiven and we are all embraced inescapably in God's love and acceptance, in spite of ourselves.

"I believe in the Holy Spirit: the holy catholic church, the communion of the saints, the forgiveness of sins, our spiritual resurrection, and the everlasting life eternal."

PART FIVE

Three Responses

19

Bible before Creed or Creed before Bible?

Jack Miles

In the gracefully learned interpretation of the Apostles' Creed and its implied pastoral theology that you have just read, J. Harold Ellens continues a dialogue that is as old as Christianity itself. His is a scriptural commentary on that creed, and as such it brings two voices together: the voice of the text and the voice of belief. His intent, I believe, is that each reader of this book should continue that dialogue in the company of friends in the faith or in the privacy of his or her own heart. What I hope to do in this brief commentary is simply to underscore the fact that there are indeed two voices to be heard.

When Jesus Christ ascended into heaven, he left no Bible behind to guide his first followers. To be sure, they had, as Jews, the Jewish Scriptures, but centuries would pass after Jesus' death, before these and the Christian additions to them would come together as the single bound volume that the word Bible now brings to mind. Moreover, even though the Jewish Scriptures, now known as *The Hebrew Bible*, included the "Books of Moses" (*Torah*), the Prophets (*Neviim*), and the Writings (*Kethuvim*), they were not official Scriptures until declared to be such in a council of Rabbis at Jamnia in 90 CE, six decades after Christ's departure.

So, even well short of the breakthrough in information technology which produced the Bible as we know it, the Jews and Jewish Christians of the first century were not in agreement about what degree of moral authority or divine authorship to attribute to the various sections of the Hebrew and Aramaic works they were reading and reciting from their

Scriptures. The terms *canon* and *canonization,* coming as they do from later Roman legal language, meant nothing to the first-century Jews and Christians.

Worst of all, the Jewish Scriptures said nothing directly about the man whom the Jewish Christians ardently believed was the awaited Jewish Messiah and perhaps much more than a messiah. How much more than a messiah? Who was to say?

When Jesus Christ ascended into heaven he left no creed behind either. He had promised a great victory over sin and death, and his resurrection was proof, however mysterious, that he could keep his promise. His original, tiny band of followers built so effectively upon that stirring promise that within three centuries the Christian church actually overwhelmed the Roman Empire. But who was the Jesus who had made the bold promise? Were his followers to employ Jewish Scripture to determine what they would believe about him, or were they to determine what would count as Scripture, past or future, by asking themselves what, collectively, they believed? As it happened, they began a conversation between the Hebrew Bible and their new faith convictions regarding Jesus. Theologians might prefer to say it was a kind of dialogue between old Jewish sacred writings and new sacred writings from the apostles.

Nothing about the Apostles' Creed is less noticed or more surprising than its utter silence about Scripture. Is Scripture authoritative because it is inspired by the Divine Spirit, or inspired even when not authoritative? Is it the word *of* God, or is it the word of men *about* God? What is its relationship to other words spoken about God or in the name of God by other saintly or ostensibly authoritative figures? The Apostles' Creed finds no need to take any particular position on such questions, and in this regard how great a contrast it makes with the 1646 Westminster Confession, that early modern Creed of the Presbyterian Churches!

That early modern confession of the faith is surely the most influential of all Reformation creeds for the English-speaking world since the sixteenth or seventeenth century. In that epoch-making confessional document, Scripture literally comes before God: In the Westminster Confession it is only after Chapter I, titled "Of the Holy Scripture," that we turn, in Chapter II, to "Of God and of the Holy Trinity." The Westminster Confession thus gives uniquely powerful expression to the view—a view that I myself do not share—that belief in the Bible grounds all other belief. Without the Bible, that confession implies, not just organized Christian worship and private Christian devotion but even belief in God would scarcely seem possible.

Yet, beyond the shadow of a doubt, organized Christian worship and private Christian devotion did exist for quite a long while before the Christian Bible came into existence. Recalling this, we might assert the right of the creed to be heard alongside the Bible, as equal in dignity and superior in antiquity. Indeed, we might well borrow the structure of a famous saying of Jesus and declare that "The Bible was made for man, not man for the Bible" (Mark 2:27).

After the Apostles' Creed, the most venerable Christian creed is the Nicene Creed; but, interestingly, the Nicene Creed is not quite as silent about Scripture as the Apostles' Creed. By the time the Council of Nicaea met, in 325 CE, a consensus was already well developed about which of the many books somehow featuring Jesus, or employing Christian or Jewish imagery, should or should not be regarded as orthodox and thus authoritative. There was, in other words, already the informal equivalent of a Christian Bible in the minds, practice, and devotion of the Christian faith communities. Perhaps it was partly for that very reason that there was a readiness for this historic council at Nicea to link the faith-formulations of the creed to the authority of Scripture.

I mean to suggest that the Christian Scriptures, the oldest of which were centuries old when the Council of Nicea convened, had been written to express the faith of those who wrote and read or heard them. Those Scriptures had already raised and answered the questions that the council would resolve by the formulation of the Nicene Creed. To take the most salient example, the gospels had spoken of a Father and a Son and a Holy Spirit, thus raising the question of the relationship among the three. To an extent, the council may be seen as a vast act of literary criticism. It tried to make summary sense of that vividly alive but sometimes fiercely contested group of texts that is the New Testament that various Christian communities prized. Very much in the manner of later literary critics, the council privileged some of those texts over others.

It is a remarkable fact that the council seems to have spent less time debating just what the contents of that emerging Bible were or should be, than they spent on formulating the creeds. This may suggest that the attending bishops were in growing agreement on the issue of what documents afloat in the church should be included in the Bible. At the very least, it suggests simply that they did not attach crucial importance to their disagreements. *The Da Vinci Code* has popularized the notion that at Nicaea Emperor Constantine replaced the existing broad-minded Bible with a new narrow-minded one of his own devising. He did nothing of the sort during the Council itself. This is not, however, to say that Constantine played no role whatsoever in the hardening of a consensus about the available documents to be chosen for the New Testament, solidifying them into a legally enforced Bible.

Had Constantine or any Roman emperor aggressively attempted to impose scriptures of his own choosing upon an unwilling church, he would have failed. This was, after all, a church with a long history of dying for its beliefs. Moreover, by Constantine's time the church dominated the empire. What Constantine did, as a patron rather than as an enemy, was, to give official certification to the generally accepted documents that made up the New Testament. As one may read in David L. Dungan's helpful new book *Constantine's Bible: Politics and the Making of the New Testament*, the emperor donated a ceremonial copy of the newly formulated Bible to each of the many imposing "royal" churches (basilicas) that he had constructed. Both the construction of the basilicas and the donation of the ceremonial Testaments that the council of bishops had decided upon, were acts not of an enemy but of the kind of overbearing friend to whom one cannot easily say "No!"

In determining the contents of the New Testament that he distributed, Constantine quite likely took his cue from the politically influential church historian Eusebius. In any case, whether out of gratitude that Christianity was no longer in danger of imperial persecution, or out of eagerness to please or, perhaps most of all out of strong motivation to conform, church leaders took out of circulation works that lacked or seemed to lack imperial sanction for inclusion in the New Testament. We are the poorer for that act of ecclesiastical and imperial censorship.

That said, the fact that this process aroused no more resistance than it did suggests that the established form of the NT already enjoyed wide acceptance. Of course, a millennium before the invention of the printing press, Scripture or written works simply did not enjoy the towering importance they would acquire in later centuries. Belief, namely personal spirituality, in those days, was the louder partner in the dialogue between the narrative of the Bible and the faith statements of the creed, just as Scripture is the louder partner today.

Within the creeds themselves, however, what importance did Scripture finally have? Let me simply make two points, each linked to one of the two modest references to Scripture that are part of the Nicene Creed as we know it, even though there are no such references to the Bible in the Apostles' Creed.

The first of these is a phrase referring to the Holy Spirit, "who with the Father and the Son is adored and glorified, *who has spoken through the prophets.*" Buried in this phrase is a *refutation* of the view, surprisingly pervasive in early Christianity, that the God whose Spirit spoke through Jesus was *not* the God who had spoken through the Jewish prophets. The second-century theologian Marcion proposed to discard the entire Old Testament on the grounds that it was clearly the work of a different deity than the one Jesus honored and identified as his Father. Comparable views were widespread in the communities whose scriptures we now call Gnostic.

It is now long ago that in order to be classified as a true Christians you had to give proof that you believed in the divine inspiration of the Old Testament. However, in the fourth century, this was still a contested matter; and a public declaration was required that one believed both testaments were from the one true and living God. That the God we know in Christ had spoken by the Jewish prophets eventually became a reproof of any antagonistic attitude toward the Jews. So there it is in the Nicene Creed.

The second reference to Scripture within the Nicene Creed is an application of the first. I refer to the insertion of the qualifying phrase "according to the Scriptures" (*secundum scripturas, kata tas graphas*) after the fateful clause "he rose from the dead." The phrase "according to the scriptures" was, I believe, a very early addition to the original Nicene Creed. It well reflects, however, the exegetical priorities of the early church in their interpretation of scripture. What mattered most about the Jewish Scriptures for the first Jewish Christians was not that they provided a guide to daily life. What mattered most was that those scriptures had predicted and thus divinely authenticated the birth, death, and resurrection of Jesus by their prophecies which were related to him as the Messiah promised in them.

However, the most interesting point of all of this lies in the fact that in the Apostles' Creed there are no such references to the Bible or to the Jewish Scriptures. Only the Hebrew metaphors of those ancient

Scriptures stand behind the words and lines of that shortest but best known of all the ancient creeds. The Apostles' Creed speaks of God as father, his uniquely begotten son, and the divine spirit. It speaks of suffering, crucifixion, death, and resurrection. It invites us to the Christian hope of God's perpetually present spirit in time and eternity. The Apostles' Creed does not reference the Bible but it attempts to mirror the Bible. Moreover, it attempts to reformulate the ancient Hebrew metaphors of Scripture in the form of the fourth-century Greek definitions of Christian Neo-Platonism.

The Jewish Scriptures that the first Christians had inherited confirmed their belief that Jesus was the Jewish Messiah and even the Jewish God Incarnate. The inherited Scriptures of the Hebrew Bible could provide that confirmation because the first Christians, as Jews, believed that the Jewish Scriptures were the word of God that foretold the coming of the Messiah. Belief told them that Scripture was divine. Scripture told them that Jesus was Lord. It is that age-old Christian conversation in which Scripture interrogates belief, and belief counter-interrogates Scripture. This is the conversation to which J. Harold Ellens invites us. It is a conversation that will last as long as humans long for the truth of God.

20

From the Apostles' Creed to Jesus' Own Trust in God

James M. Robinson

I AM PLEASED TO write this guest chapter in Dr. Ellens' fine book. He has just analyzed for us the historic message of the faith of the church as set forth in the Apostles' Creed and its implications for the continuing work of the divine spirit in the world. He has critiqued that tradition of faith and teaching in the light of the gospels of the New Testament. He has also applied its message in numerous practical ways to everyday Christian life.

I assume that you all know what the Christian gospel of the *church* is, namely what the Christian church has always used as its central message: *Jesus died for our sins and rose from the dead on the third day.* You may not, however, realize how different the Church's tradition of faith really is from the actual message of Jesus himself. That is, you may not have had the opportunity to learn to what extent you do not know the actual gospel of *Jesus* himself. For his message was not that *he died for our sins and rose again from the dead on the third day.* What then was *his* message?

THE APOSTLES' CREED

This gap in our knowledge about Jesus is made painfully clear by the Apostles' Creed, which most of you know by heart. It begins with what was done *for* Jesus, "conceived by the Holy Spirit, born of the Virgin Mary," and then skips to what was done *against* Jesus, "suffered under Pontius Pilate, was crucified, dead, and buried." But you may not have noticed, even with Dr. Ellens careful explication of the creed, that what is skipped in the middle of the creed is what was done *by* Jesus, as if it were not important enough to include in what we believe *about* Jesus. Did Jesus do or say nothing worth believing between Bethlehem and Golgotha? He most surely did! That is what I want to lay out in this epilogue to the illumining reflections on the Apostles' Creed, so ably developed by my friend and colleague, The Reverend Dr. J. Harold Ellens. I want to set forth what was really Jesus' own take on the gospel, that is, the good news, he wanted to give us.

THE MISSION INSTRUCTIONS

Perhaps the best way to get at this in very concrete terms is to begin with what has usually been called the mission instructions that Jesus gave his disciples when he sent them out. This is a particularly old bit of tradition. It is preserved in two independent drafts, one in Mark and one in Q, a collection of sayings of Jesus imbedded in Matthew and Luke. Mark was the gospel of the Gentile Church, and so made some concessions to fit the mission in the wider Gentile world. Some of these concessions were permitting one to wear sandals and carry a club for protection, as the disciples went out on their mission journeys. These provisions are absent from the Q parallel, since Q was the gospel of the Jewish Church, which continued Jesus' mission among Jewish villages in Galilee. It is fair to assume that the mission instructions Jesus gave in Q give us the oldest record we have of Jesus' own practice in Galilee.

Of course, we should not assume that Jesus stood up in front of the apostles and made a speech like the mission instructions. Rather let us assume the mission instructions are really a rather reliable record of what Jesus and his disciples actually did during his public ministry in Galilee. That is why we begin with them (Q 10:2-9):

> He said to his disciples: The harvest is plentiful, but the workers are few. So ask the Lord of the harvest to dispatch workers into his harvest. Be on your way! Look, I send you like sheep in the midst of wolves. Carry no purse, nor knapsack, nor shoes, nor stick, and greet no one on the road. Into whatever house you enter, first say: Peace to this house! If a son of peace is there, let your peace come upon him; but if not, let your peace return upon you. At that house remain, eating and drinking whatever they provide, for the worker is worthy of his or her reward. Do not move around from

house to house; and whatever town you enter and they take you in, eat what is set before you, and cure the sick there, and say to them: God's reign has reached unto you.

Here already we strike upon the key term of Jesus' whole public ministry. We are used to talking about it as "the kingdom of God," but it is more accurately understood as "God's reign," or "God reigning." This is the only idiom in all the sayings of Jesus that could be considered in any way a theological term. So let me pause to show how it functions in the mission instructions: Once you knock on a door and call out *Shalom*, and the son of peace admits you for what we today might call bed and breakfast, they serve you dinner and you heal their sick. Jesus interprets this as God reigning in that house (Q 10:9b). The disciples are to say to that household, "God's reign has reached unto you."

A story at the beginning of Jesus' public ministry in Capernaum makes this concrete (Mark 1:29–31): "Immediately he left the synagogue, and entered the house of Simon and Andrew, with James and John. Now Simon's mother-in-law lay sick with a fever, and immediately they told him of her; and he came and took her by the hand and lifted her up, and the fever left her, and she served them." Here one can see in practice the combination of Jesus or his disciples healing and receiving bed and breakfast.

Faith Healing

We begin with the healing of the sick as God reigning: Jesus was in fact what we today would call a faith healer, since in a number of healing stories Jesus emphasized the faith of those he heals. The story of the healing of the centurion's boy probably goes back to a real healing by Jesus, since it is the only healing in Q (7:1–10), and is also told independently in the Gospel of John (4:46b–54). Here the centurion's faith is explicitly praised (Q 7:9b): "Not even in Israel have I found such faith."

Four other healing stories include Jesus' comment, "Your faith has healed you" (Mark 5:34 par. Matt 9:22 par. Luke 8:48; Mark 10:52 par. Luke 18:42; Luke 7:50; 17:19). Moreover, there are a number of other instances of faith being the condition for a healing, e.g., Mark 9:22b–24: The anguished father of the sick child cried out, "If you can do anything, have pity on us and help us." Then Jesus said to him, "'If you can?' All things are possible to him who believes!" Immediately the father of the child cried out and said, "I believe; help my unbelief!" Other such associations of faith with healings make it abundantly clear that *faith healer* is an accurate description of Jesus.

However, one must be clear what *faith healer* means: It does not mean that the healer is the one who has faith, but rather it is the one wanting to be healed who is to have faith. Jesus tells the sick that it is their faith that will heal them, not his prowess as a faith healer. Jesus did not present faith healing as his own action, but as God reigning in the lives of those who trust God. It even took place when it was someone other than himself who was doing the cure (Q 11:20–21): "And if I by Beelzebub cast out demons, your sons, by whom do they cast them out? This is why they will be your judges; but if it is by the finger of God that I cast out demons, then there has come upon you God's reign."

Demon Possession

This then brings us to illnesses that were considered to be demon possession. Some sicknesses went beyond the normal symptoms of having to lie in bed, too weak to get up and get around, like Peter's mother-in-law. Demon possessions showed themselves by the reverse symptoms, namely getting around excessively (Mark 9:17b–18a, 20–22, 26):

> He has a dumb spirit; and wherever it seizes him, it dashes him down; and he foams and grinds his teeth and becomes rigid. . . . And they brought the boy to him; and when the spirit saw him, immediately it convulsed the boy, and he fell on the ground and rolled about, foaming at the mouth. And Jesus asked his father, "How long has he had this?" And he said, "From childhood. And it has often cast him into the fire and into the water, to destroy him; . . . And after crying out and convulsing him terribly, it came out, and the boy was like a corpse.

Of course, they did not know how to explain what we might call epileptic seizures. Matthew uses a participial that means "moon-struck" (Matt 17:15; also Matt 4:24—The Revised Standard Version has modernized this phrase by translating it as epileptic). In Matthew's world of thought, epilepsy could be explained as being moon-struck. The more common term for such seizures, used by Mark (9:17) in telling the same story, is "deaf and dumb spirit." "Spirit," Greek *pneuma*, is the same Greek word that is used for "wind" or "breeze." We all know that there are bad winds, such as hurricanes, blizzards, tempests, gales, tornados. Such a bad wind, at the individual level, they called an evil spirit. In this story it is an evil spirit that prevented the poor epileptic boy from speaking.

A synonym for evil spirit is "demon." This term originally meant a minor deity or a power (a daimon), but got demoted to just an evil spirit. They understood that it could enter a person and take over that person's mind and body. So when the human talked, they thought it was really the demon talking; and they were sure that what the poor person's body did, such as having convulsions, was due to the demon torturing him.

Jesus stood up to such a demon, and the poor epileptic snapped out of his seizure, and fell to the ground as if dead. For the on-lookers, nothing could be a more dramatic proof of Jesus' own superhuman powers! It is interesting, and no doubt important, that Jesus explained this not in terms of him being something special in his own person, but as God reigning in what he did (Q 11:20): "If it is by the finger of God that I cast out demons, then there has come upon you God's reign."

Thus we have two very archaic sayings that speak of God reigning in the case of healings, one when he was admitted for bed and breakfast and healed the sick there, the other when he snapped the epileptic out of his seizure. These two sayings are generally considered to be reports that most surely go back to Jesus himself, and so define most clearly what he was talking about when he used his one-and-only theological category, "the kingdom of God."

He did not have in mind what this term suggests to us today, namely, a geographical area with citizens of that kingdom, a translation that has had devastating political implications: The Crusades took back the Holy Land from the "infidels," to set up there "the kingdom of God." In modern times, one can think of Christendom as "the kingdom of God": The British Empire on which in its heyday the sun never set, the Holy Roman Empire of the German Nation which made the Kaiser into Caesar, and Manifest Destiny which gave the West of North America to the United States. Though all this empire-building was carried out in the name of "the kingdom of God," it flies in the face of all that Jesus had to say. Yet it all happened with the church's blessing. So we should stop talking about the political category of "the kingdom of God," as an area of control. Instead we should focus on the spiritual category of God reigning in us or in God's world, if we want to understand Jesus.

Food

There is still another dimension to God reigning, according to the sayings of Jesus. When admitted into a house for bed and breakfast by one who was worthy to be called a "son of peace," two things happened that Jesus explained as God reigning: He 1) received an evening meal and 2) he healed the sick. It may seem to us more obvious to think of God reigning in the healing of the sick than in the evening meal, but that is because we are fortunate enough that we do not need to think in terms of the basic necessities of life. We are not in a situation like the disciples were in their day, often wondering what they would eat and what they would drink. We can take food for granted in our time and culture. However, when you do not know where your next meal is coming from, and then you get fed out of the blue, you thank God for anything you get to eat and sense it as a providential gift from God, indicating that God reigns there and in that event.

So let me explain. Jesus had renounced taking with him on the road the basic necessities of life, and so had neither a purse for money to buy supplies, nor a backpack to take supplies along with him. Instead, his solution was just to pray for food. We are all familiar with his prayer, but we may not realize how much it is a prayer for food. The petition we recite as "Thy kingdom come" means "Let your reign come." But Matthew's church introduced at this point a petition that was not originally in the prayer, and which interrupted the original flow of the prayer itself: Matthew's petition "thy will be done on earth as it is in heaven" is not in Luke's version of the prayer. But here it is Luke which is nearer to Q and thus to Jesus. So, in Jesus' prayer, "Let your reign come" continued directly into: "Our day's bread give us today." Food is the first and major implementation of God's reign happening in the here and how.

When Jesus and his followers were admitted to a house for bed and breakfast, God was reigning in the food they were given just as much as in the healings they performed. When Jesus pronounced on the house (Q 10:9b), "God's reign has reached unto you," he meant both that they had responded to God's call on them to help the visitors with food, and they had received from God what they needed, namely, the healings. For God reigning cuts both ways: God motivates others to help us, and motivates us to help others.

Jesus reassured his followers that God would indeed provide food for them—they need only call on him and trust him to respond (Q 11:7–

13). "I tell you: Ask and it will be given to you, search and you will find, knock and it will be opened to you. For everyone who asks, receives, and the one who searches, finds, and to the one who knocks it will be opened. What person of you, whose child asks for bread, will give him a stone? Or again when he asks for a fish, will give him a snake? So if you though evil know how to give good gifts to your children, by how much more will the Father from heaven give good things to those who ask him?"

Jesus did not mean that bread and fish will fall like manna from heaven for the disciples, but rather that God will motivate some "son of peace" to take them in, when they knock, for bed and breakfast. Rather than being anxiety-laden about where the next square meal is coming from, one should trust God to provide it, just as do the birds (Q 12:24). "Consider the ravens: They neither sow nor reap nor gather into barns, and yet God feeds them. Are you not better than the birds?" This boils down to the Beatitude of Jesus (Q 6:21a): "Blessed are you who hunger, for you will eat your fill."

Clothing

The same is true of the other minimal necessities of life, such as clothing (Q 12:27–28). "Observe the lilies: They do not card nor do they spin. Yet I tell you, not even Solomon in all his glory was arrayed like one of these. But if in the field the grass, there today and tomorrow thrown into the oven, God clothes thus, will he not much more clothe you, persons of petty faith!" So, for Jesus, *faith* means trust in God for the basic necessities of life, not a battery of beliefs like the Apostles' Creed (Q 12: 22b, 29–30). "Therefore I tell you: Do not be anxious about your life, what you are to eat, nor about your body, in what you are to clothe yourself.... So do not be anxious, saying: What are we to eat, or What are we to drink, or What are we to wear? For all these the Gentiles seek; for your Father knows that you need them all." This again is God reigning (Q 12:31): "But seek his reign, and all these shall be granted to you." This boils down to the Beatitude of Jesus (Q 6:20b): "Blessed are you poor, for yours is the kingdom of God."

Jesus' Ethics

You trusting God to motivate someone to provide your basic necessities of life goes along with God motivating you to provide just such necessities for someone else (Q 6:30). "To the one who asks of you, give; and from the one who borrows, do not ask back what is yours." We are tempted to say that the dregs of society do not deserve all this loving tender care! What did they ever do for us? They just live off us as long as they can, and then move on to the next sucker! You can love your neighbor (Mark 12:31a), whom you have known all your life, and you know that your neighbor loves you, and would help you out in a pinch. But those street people!

That is not what Jesus had in mind by repeating the familiar biblical injunction to love one's neighbor, which can all too readily be limited to one's own class, or tribe, or race, or religion, or neighborhood. That is not what Jesus meant at all (Q 6:32, 34). "If you love those loving you, what reward do you have? Do not even the tax collectors [thieves] do the same? And if you lend to those from whom you hope to receive, what reward do you have? Do not even the Gentiles do the same?"

He had to explain by telling the parable of the Good Samaritan (Luke 10:29–37), since for centuries Samaritans had been the most obvious enemies of the Jews: When a Jew falls among thieves who left him half-dead in the gutter, it was not his fellow-Jews who come to his aid, but the despised Samaritan, who thereby showed that he loved even his enemy in need.

This then is what loving your neighbor meant to Jesus (Q 6:27–28, 35c–d): "Love your enemies and pray for those persecuting you, so that you may become sons of your Father, for he raises his sun on the bad and the good and rains on the just and the unjust." This is a completely new revelation of God, which transcends the God who calls on you to retaliate by the law of the jungle by tooth and claw, as Matthew makes clear (Matt 5:38–42). "You have heard that it was said, "An eye for an eye and a tooth for a tooth." But I say to you, 'Do not resist one who is evil. For if any one strikes you on the right cheek, turn to him the other also; and if any one would sue you and take your coat, let him have your cloak as well; and if any one forces you to go one mile, go with him two miles. Give to him who begs from you, and do not refuse him who would borrow from you.'"

Jesus called on his followers to forsake the age-old legal tradition of a just revenge, in favor of his new revelation of an all-forgiving God (Q 10:21–22). Justice is not the solution, Jesus teaches. We must go far beyond justice to love, mercy, and grace. "I praise you, Father, Lord of heaven and earth, for you hid these things from sages and the learned, and disclosed them to children. Yes, Father, for that is what it has pleased you to do. Everything has been entrusted to me by my Father, and no one knows ... the Father except the Son, and to whomever the Son chooses to reveal him."

Easter

What is most glaringly absent from the Sayings Gospel Q are the Christmas story and Holy Week, culminating in the Easter narrative. Of course, as the modern secularization and commercialization of Christmas and Easter make clear to thinking Christians, what is at issue in Christmas and Easter is not the trappings, but the substance. Perhaps Q does have the substance of the Easter faith, if indeed that substance is more than angels singing carols at his birth and moving stones at his tomb. According to Q, the substance of Christmas and Easter is that, in spite of all appearances to the contrary, God is here, acting for our good in our lives, taking care of us, and sending us out to care for others, thereby giving our lives ultimate meaning.

The crucifixion must have been simply terrible to witness, seeing a loved one hanging there in excruciating pain, hour after hour, with cold-blooded soldiers from the army of occupation casually standing guard lest you approach and try to help. The realization must have come crashing down upon the disciples, if they had any common sense at all, that Jesus' life's quest had been a wonderful dream that had nothing to do with reality. They had no choice but to give up trying to "fish for people" and so they returned to Galilee to resume fishing for fish.

Yet Jesus' death was not the last word, for the Sayings Gospel Q belies that obvious assertion! It was only after Jesus' crucifixion that all his trusting words about a caring heavenly Father were repeated, collected, and recorded by his disciples in Q, ultimately to reach us in Matthew and Luke in the New Testament. Moreover, this took place not as a nostalgic, sad memory of what they had so hoped might be true, but now they knew was much too good to be true.

Quite the contrary! They began all over again to proclaim Jesus' message, as if nothing could happen, not even the worst, to shake their faith. Jesus' faith had survived the beheading of John, Jesus' mentor; and the disciples' faith survived the crucifixion of Jesus, their master. They still heard him saying: "What I say to you in the dark, speak in the light;

and what you hear whispered in the ear, proclaim on the housetops. Do not be afraid of those who kill the body, but cannot kill the soul." What matters is integrity, not external circumstances or even life span. They realized that what Jesus said was still true, even in the most desperate of situations!

It is neither the empty tomb nor the resurrection appearances that created the Easter faith. It is, rather, the other way around. This may come as a bit of a surprise, so let me try to illustrate it from our modern experience of Christmas and Easter with our children. We know how to tell our children that the Christmas tree and Santa Claus do not make Christmas, that it is the other way around: Jesus' birthday makes them! Also, if Jesus had not been raised from the dead, there would be no Easter rabbit or Easter eggs. So we cannot lose sight of Jesus' birth and resurrection, which is too easy to do (and not only for children), flooded as we are with all the advertisements for what is on sale at such holidays.

Just as we tell our children that they must think behind the trappings to the substance of Christmas and Easter, just so as adults we must think more deeply. It is not the resurrection stories that made Easter, but the other way around. It was his disciples experiencing Jesus still scoring his point, as a gospel still real even after his death, which created the Easter stories. So that is the only valid form of Christian faith today. Easter faith is taking Jesus at his word that God is a heavenly Father who really cares, who reigns *for us* and *through us* in our daily lives. Easter was not just the launching of another religion of a dying and rising God, of which the ancient world had too many already. It was the disciples' renewed experience of Jesus saying all over again that God continues to be here *for us*, and *for others through us*, in spite of the horror of "Good" Friday. This is indeed good news, the gospel of Jesus risen from the dead and forever present to us in the Divine Spirit. That is why the Apostles' Creed closes with that important and intensely believable line, "I believe in the Holy Spirit, the holy catholic church, the communion of saints, the forgiveness of sins, and the life everlasting."

CONCLUSION

We began with the Apostles' Creed, and tried to fill in the gap between what was done *for* Jesus and what was done *against* Jesus, by focusing on what was said and done *by* Jesus. This has led to Jesus' revelation of a new kind of all-forgiving God, in whom we are invited to have complete trust. So we can say that our understanding of what a follower of Jesus is supposed to believe has moved beyond the Apostles' Creed to Jesus' own trust in God.

21

A Pastor's Response

F. Morgan Roberts

I STILL REMEMBER THE sense of discovery that I experienced when I read the first draft of this book. It was much shorter than this final version, consisting mainly of what J. Harold Ellens termed "homiletical reflections" upon the creed. With clarity, authority, and scholarly insight, he had given expression to convictions I had held for many years. When, sometime later, he asked me if I would write a few words of recommendation for the book jacket, I was delighted to be even so small a part of this important work. Now, many months later, I have the even greater honor of adding this pastoral response to the finished work.

It is fitting that this final word be a "pastor's response" because the final product seems to me, above all, essentially pastoral. In the beginning, I might have expected that the principal goal was to engage the reader in theological reflection; however, what has emerged is a book that calls us, in a pastoral spirit, to a new way of life. More than about beliefs, this book is calling us to an entirely challenging way of living. Let me try to express the sense of liberation that I hope you have experienced as you have read this book and reflected upon this "godly way of life" that Dr. Ellens proposes.

In his book *If the Church Were Christian*,[1] Quaker pastor Philip Gulley tells how, in the hometown of his childhood, there was a man who built an intricate and expansive model railroad village in the basement of this house. The layout filled the basement and, along with the trains,

---

1. Philip Gulley, *If the Churches were Christian: Recovering the Values of Jesus* (New York: HarperCollins, 2010) 173.

there were houses, streets, stores, trees, lakes, mountains, and whatever else might make it an entire world of its own. When children learned of this Toyland they began to arrive at the man's front door, begging for a tour of his enchanted world. Indeed, enchantment is just the right word for what was happening to the man who made this model world. As the man made his railroad town larger and larger, his real life upstairs slowly fell apart with lack of care. The upkeep of his house, lawn, and garden was neglected. He became addicted to his fantasy world in his basement. It became more real to him than what should have been his real world. Worse yet, his relationships with family and friends finally just died.

Philip Gulley uses the image of this man's basement world to talk about that alternative reality that the church has fashioned, that fanciful theological world in the church's mind that has distracted it from the realities of the actual world in which the church is called to ministry and mission. Let me, in my own terms, express how I understand that imaginary, basement village world that has distracted the church from the life of joyful service in the real world, to which it is called. Dr. Ellens has given us here a book that exposes the shaky foundations upon which this fanciful world in the church's mind has been constructed.

For centuries, a major portion of the church has confused the game going on in the basement with reality. Christians have been so captivated by this basement game that we are mostly out of touch with what is really happening in the world of our daily lives. It is only by an uncritical cherry-picking of selected verses from scripture that this imaginary world has been constructed. Moreover, the main theme of this fanciful game is the notion that the meaning of everything in heaven and earth is that God is caught up in a cosmic warfare with the forces of evil and we better get on board one side of the other.

With the kind of craze that *Dungeons and Dragons* once created on college campuses, a majority of Christians actually believe that the real world is the one in which this cosmic battle surrounds their life and the life of the world at large. They believe that the battleground of God's cosmic fight with the devil is human history and the human heart.

The main players in this great battle are God and Satan, who seem to possess equal power as the representatives of ultimate good and ultimate evil. When the eventual outcome of this battle is described, it is as though the two are evenly matched for a genuine contest. Satan will not be completely defeated. He will be able to destroy a lot of things in God's world, and he will carry away the spoils of the battle in the form of hosts of humans he has captured, and he will be able to keep them forever. In this cosmic warfare, God is battling to draw the souls of humankind to his side so that they will finally live with him victoriously in heaven, while Satan is battling to draw those same souls to his side and, eventually, down into his own realm of hell, where they will be tormented forever. Satan is never a total loser; he will carry away some souls with him into the lake of fire, forever. God will not come away from this battle as a total winner because not even God can guarantee the salvation of every child of his creation. The stakes in this battle are very high, indeed; and very final.

In this historic worldview in the mind of the church, this war has been going on since the beginning days of creation when our original parents were deceived by Satan in the guise of a serpent. Adam and Eve disobeyed the rules and regulations about life in Paradise Park, the lovely garden that God had established for his children. After this fall from their original state of innocence, many centuries passed before a solution was found for correcting the situation. God could not just overlook what had been done; sin had to be punished, and God's wrath against that sin had to be vented upon all humanity.

It turns out in the church's story, however, that God had a Son and this Son was more sympathetic to our human predicament. At some moment in eternity, God's Son agreed to come down to earth, become one of us, and allow himself to be killed in our place. When God decided on this proposition he was suspending his own law against child sacrifice. Since God was so angry that he just wanted to kill somebody, God allowed his Son to be a child-sacrifice for us. So the story goes that God vented his wrath upon Jesus, instead of us. The church has always called that deal the substitutionary sacrifice that provided a solution to our predicament. Of course, the sacrifice frees us only if, believing in our hearts that Jesus has taken our place, we accept him as our substitute. If we do, our debt is paid and we go to heaven. If not, we go to hell with the Devil and his fallen angels.

That, stated briefly, is the epitome of the cosmic battle that is constantly raging, and always surrounding our life in this world. When this plan of salvation is proclaimed from sophisticated pulpits, it is usually enhanced by genteel modifications and theological qualifications. However, whether this fanciful theological worldview is proclaimed by some priest in high-church regalia as he administers the sacrament, saying, "The body of Christ is broken for you, the blood of Christ is shed for you;" or whether we read the words, "Christ died for our sins," painted upon some farmer's barn in the Christ-haunted Bible Belt, the bottom line is the same. Both the high churchman and the Bible-believing Baptist are captives of the same basement game, the church's alternative world of reality, its dramatic cosmic battle in which we are all involved.

There is, of course, and entirely different, scriptural interpretation of the meaning of Jesus' death in which it becomes a demonstration of God's radical, unlimited, and universal grace. However, my experience during half a century of pastoral ministry is that the vast majority of Christians, Catholic, Protestant, Baptist, or Orthodox, understand spiritual reality in terms of that fanciful cosmic battle. They hold to the basement village notion that we can be saved from the wrath of God, the wiles of Satan, and the eternal torments of hell by believing in the substitutionary atoning death of Jesus. That's the basement game that has captivated the hearts and minds of most people who call themselves Christians.

As I write these words, I am rather sure that some readers have not stayed with us until this last chapter. They stopped reading in the early chapters when they discovered that the Dr. Ellens has terminated the Devil's employment and closed the death camp of hell. For some people, Christian faith without Satan and hell is impossible. However, for those of you who have stayed with us this far, let me offer a special invitation. Consider what an addiction to the basement game can do to the hearts and minds of those who somehow cannot escape its enchantment. I invite you to ponder five questions as you think back upon what you have read in this book:

1. Does anyone live convincingly as though they actually believe in the cosmic battle?

2. Do those who profess belief in the Evangelicals' plan of salvation, a central feature of the cosmic battle, realize what violence they are attributing to the nature of God?

3. Does the cosmic battle game make those who are addicted to it sick people?

4. What happens to preachers who make the basement game the essence of their ministry—their reality?

5. Has the basement game become a pervasive addictive form of American entertainment?

Let me share with you where those questions carried my mind as I read this book.

1. *Does anyone live convincingly as though they actually believe in this cosmic battle?* How could anyone possibly live a reasonably happy Christian life while harboring such beliefs? Am I really to believe that, right now, as I write these words, many former family members and friends are screaming in torments—torments infinitely worse than anything Hitler could ever have conceived and carried out? Indeed, according to such a fantasy theology, most of the Jews who suffered Hitler's atrocities went immediately into something fiendishly worse when they died in the concentration camps. They went straight into God's death ovens. They simply had not accepted Jesus as the substitutionary sacrifice for their sins.

What you will notice is that there are many Christians who say that they believe in hell, while in actual practice, they live as though such a nightmarish reality does not exist. They go on spending their time and money on cruises, parties, and worldly diversions as though there were no hell. They live, work, eat, drink, play golf and tennis with unbelieving friends and colleagues who are literally living on the cliff's edge of hell, so to speak. At any moment, some accident could carry their next door neighbor into the lake of fire. If they really believed in hell, they could hardly sleep at night in concern for their lost neighbors. They would flinch at no effort necessary to warn their neighbors of their impending torment. The fact is that they do not really believe in hell's literal existence. If they did, they would be living differently than they do. Does it not require the cauterization of ones conscience and schizoid division of ones mind to believe one way and live quite differently? For ordinary, decent folk who attend churches where they are trained to think in terms of the fictional basement game of cosmic conflict, it becomes almost impossible for them to exist without resorting to groundless rationalizations to justify their professed beliefs.

I can remember a devout fundamentalist banker whose wife did not attend his true-believer church. She lived what seemed to him to be a worldly life, playing cards, attending movies, smoking, and enjoying the very pleasures that he had renounced for the sake of bearing witness to his faith. Despite the handwriting on the wall that clearly indicated the eternally fatal direction toward which her life was moving, he confided in me that he was sure that "down deep" in her heart she was really a believer. The thought of his wife writhing in eternal torments was unthinkable. Figuring out how to witness effectively to her, seemed to him impossible. Interestingly, hell is always for those "other" people; never for our own loved ones. We have all visited funeral homes where we have heard bereaved believers deny what their fundamentalist faith teaches, forcing some other part of their mind to believe that their departed loved one is really in heaven, even when there is incontrovertible evidence that the dead person did not share a shred of their fundamentalist faith.

Of course, there are many decent people who are somehow better than their system of belief. Even though their church teaches them that true Christian faith demands the existence of the Devil and the necessity of an eternal hell, they somehow rise above the dark implications of this hellish faith in their daily lives. They hold somewhat to the fanciful alternate world view of the church, but they live in terms of a different literal reality. Does this not indicate that God has built a basic integrity into our human nature, so that it is only with herculean effort that our minds can be forced to accept what our hearts reject. When we observe how impossible it is for those who profess belief in the cosmic battle to live consistently and convincingly with the practical implications of their belief system, it indicates that the need for psycho-spiritual wholeness is built into our nature. Persistent abuse of this inherent need for wholeness, however, will finally produce a deeply fractured soul, a profoundly sick person. The overwhelming evidence from the lives of ordinary people seems to be that, despite what some Christians say they believe, hardly anyone really believes in the cosmic battle or their having a role in it on God's side or the Devil's.

2. *Do those who profess belief in the Evangelical Fundamentalist plan of salvation, a central feature of the cosmic battle, realize what violence they are attributing to the nature of God?* What kind of a God would need to kill someone, almost anyone who happens to be handy, for the purpose of relieving his anger? Worse yet, what kind of a father would kill his own son to discharge the wrath he feels toward someone who has wronged him? Yet the cast of characters in the doctrine of the substitutionary atonement demands the existence of God as such an "unheav-

enly" father. Week after week, in church after church, such bad news is proclaimed as the good news of the gospel!

When such a sick gospel is proclaimed, I am asked to believe that I was born with a spiritually diseased nature, with an inherent affliction called sin. I did not ask to be born, and I did not contract this disease by any willful or careless act of my own. I was just born that way. Yet I am told that God will torture me forever if I do not accept the substitute sacrifice that he has provided for me in the death of Jesus. What kind of God would hate me with such intensity for the sin of having been born, or for somebody else's sin? What real choice do I have other than to accept God's offer in craven *fear*? Could I *love* such a God? Never! It is not in our nature to love a God whose behavior is sicker than that of the world's most demented and vicious killers.

As easily and glibly as this sick message is regularly proclaimed, from the pulpits of Bible-believing churches, and in many traditional prayers of liturgical churches, it is striking how ordinary folk never seem to ask the obvious question. "Whatever happened to the loving heavenly Father about whom I was taught in my early Sunday School lessons?" Why is it that we never ask, "Whatever happened to the heavenly Father in whom Jesus had such radical trust, the God whom Jesus called Abba (daddy), the loving Father of the Sermon on the Mount?"

There is, however, a theological rationale by which basically decent people remain in such churches and continue to participate in the basement game of that divine and demonic cosmic battle. We stay in the game by focusing our faith upon Jesus, our real friend, and by allowing the tyrannical Father to fade out into his typical role in the violent Old Testament stories. It is remarkable how many Christians believe that the God of the Old Testament is a different, harsher God than the kind divinity we experience in Jesus. It is no accident that the most well-known hymn of American Christianity is "Jesus loves me." Jesus has, understandably, taken over the role of the loving God for most Christians. Christian bookstores sell simple plastic picture frames imprinted with the word, "Jesus loves." You can mount pictures of your children in them. Why Jesus? Does God not love children? Evidently not, because we all, even non-Christians, sing, "Jesus loves the little children; all the children of the world." The "praise songs" sing repetitively about Jesus. Evidently, the heavenly Father is out of a job. Quite appropriately, a Methodist theologian recently wrote an important article in a church magazine. She entitled it, "What ever happened to the Father?"

That some of the members of our churches keep returning, week after week, to be abused by sermons in which such a violent God is portrayed, seems indicative of the same kind of sickness that keeps battered spouses in abusive marriages. This is a sickness that continues to afflict them even after they have left such sick marriages.

3. *Does the cosmic battle game make those who are addicted to it sick people?* My immediate answer is a resounding "yes." However, I want to be fair and cautious as we discuss this question. We have already noted that many people, of any theological outlook, are actually better people than their theology would lead them to be. There are simple souls who are subjected weekly to sermons from a "hell fire and damnation" pulpit who, nonetheless, are kinder and gentler folk than their preacher's rantings would lead them to become. Thankfully, people seldom practice fully what their preacher preaches.

Overall, however, it is fairly well established that sick religion makes sick people. People who believe in a cruel God are inhaling a spiritually polluted air that can make them cruel people. People who believe in a God who would endlessly torture any one of his children can become people who condone cruel and unusual punishment of enemies. People who believe in an eternal hell in which there is no hope of pardon and from which there is no escape, can become people with little concern for the just treatment of prisoners. People who believe that, at the end of life, God gives up forever on those who have failed and disposes of them as trash, can become people who decide that certain people in our world may be treated as trash.

The seriousness of the sickness that sick religion can produce will vary from patient to patient, but the sickness will be real. Even in the best case scenario, a sick belief system will breed a general indifference toward selected groups and persons who are simply too much trouble to be bothered with. It is such religious sickness that allows many Christians to "pass by on the other side," in the name of their sick religious beliefs.

A particular image comes to my mind when I think of people whose understanding of Christian faith keeps them involved in the fanciful basement game of false theology. I think of those sad souls who sit in windowless gambling casinos, playing the same purposeless games, hour after hour, wasting precious time and money that could be enjoyed healthfully, or contributed charitably in the sunlit world outside the casino. What a waste to spend ones life in such a game. How much worse that an equally addictive game of the false theology of a terrorizing God should become the essence of Christian life for those who play the cosmic battle game in the spiritual basements of their souls!

4. *What happens to preachers who make the basement game the essence of their ministry?* What happens to pastors who actively promote this kind of addictive religion? I have known preachers who actually believed more devoutly in the existence of hell than they believed in the existence of God. The existence of hell is the bottom line of their faith; indeed, hell is their reason for being in the ministry of the church.

Many years ago I read the missionary application form for a nondenominational mission society. Applicants had to subscribe to the usual "fundamentals" of evangelical faith. However, the most important issue was that they had to subscribe to the statement that the "heathen" would be eternally lost without faith in Christ. Hell was the *sine qua non* of their theology. There was no reason to be a missionary if one did not believe in a well populated hell!

Many Christian pastors function upon the same basis. Without hell there is no reason for entering the ministry. If there is no hell, there is no urgent reason for preaching their so-called "gospel." Their practice of ministry is an eternalized version of selling fire insurance. So many of them become lifeless and stale in retirement! If they were honest, they would admit that they are tired of having to sell the same old fire insurance policy day after day, sermon after sermon, Sunday after Sunday. Such preachers, when retired, seem to lose all interest in learning and exploring matters of faith. For them there is nothing more to explore, nothing more to learn. They have resigned and passed their sales territory and customers on to the next generation of salesmen. Their interests are now in golf and their hobbies. One of them whom I know thought it was rather weird that at age 82 I still try to read some portion of the Greek New Testament every day. When preachers believe more deeply in hell than in the loving Father of whom Jesus spoke, it is as though the God of amazing, universal grace, the God whose loving providence marks even the fall of a sparrow, is not a sufficient motivation for their ministry or life.

5. *Has the basement game become a pervasive, addictive form of American entertainment?* A final aspect of the sickness engendered by the cosmic battle game is the pervasive effect that it has upon society outside of the church. There are so many churches in which that catastrophic apocalyptic message of the terrorizing God is standard fare. Think of the many radio and TV ministries devoted to such a message. I suspect that there is a general public perception that this morbid message is what the Christian faith is about. Witness, for example, the high percentage of persons who, when polled about religious matters, profess to believe that the time of Christ's return, the cataclysmic judgment day, and the end of the world is imminent. Public opinion is also influenced by the large number of persons who, though they are no longer affiliated with the church, continue to think of the Christian faith in such fanciful terms. It is as though the church's doomsday game still has an inescapable grip upon their minds.

It is interesting that I receive emails from such former church members and discover that they have found another sphere in which they can continue to think and live apocalyptically; but without the time and expense of church membership. Their new gaming place is the internet where they consume hours every day, visiting websites that perpetuate the kind of conspiratorial thinking characteristic of the demonic cosmic battle mentality. The political internet prophets tell them that "the time is near," assuring them that society is on the verge of a sinister takeover. The message can come from the political right or left, but the message is essentially and psychologically the same: the false sick paranoid notion that forces of evil are seeking to destroy our society, and so forth.

Sometimes the message is given a religious spin on the Internet, calling for a return to the "old time religion" or to the faith of the "founding fathers." However, the Internet prophet is still sounding the same call to wake up and join the battle. Some of these websites are unquestionably sick and downright dangerous, especially those that fan the flames of racial hatred and issue an actual call to arms. My general pastoral concern, however, is for those families in which marriages or relationships with children are deteriorating because of the fact that some spouse is addictively engrossed by such political apocalypticism. The basement game does not make us kinder, gentler people. Better it would be that such addicts devoted themselves to model railroading!

Here then is Dr. Ellens' important book that summons us to leave the basement and its distracting, destructive game, and to begin living upstairs in the light and life of the Spirit-filled world. There the God of radical, universal, unconditional, and unlimited grace is alive and well. After you have had time to reflect upon my five questions, the most important issue becomes: How Then Shall I Live?

A preacher's life during 50 years can be an exciting pilgrimage, especially when one decides to resign from the eternal fire insurance business. I was ten years into my ministry when I stopped peddling that insurance. I began to believe in God's radical, unconditional, and universal grace. I set out to learn what it would mean to live my life and carry on my ministry in the joy and challenge of such a faith. One of my important friends along the way was my fellow sojourner, J. Harold Ellens. Perhaps the best way to describe what I have learned through my journey is to describe what has become for me an ordinary day's sojourn.

Upon awakening each morning, I often recall the opening words of the old hymn, "This Is My Father's World." This may not be the greatest hymn in the world but those words are so spiritually wholesome and assuring. I find them much more spiritually healing than Luther's morose lines in "A Mighty Fortress is Our God." Luther wrote, "And though this world, with devils filled, Should threaten to undo us." I choose not believe that this world is dominated by the "Prince of Darkness grim" and his minions.

It is true that the gospels occasionally though rarely present Jesus as going "head-to-head" with Satan. However, in the New Testament era, when the religious mind was drenched in Enochic Apocalyptic Judaism, it was inevitable that the story of Jesus would be told in such terms as well. A critical reading of scripture, however, releases me from bondage to that ancient mythology. After all, Satan is a late import from other cultures and does not appear in Hebrew scripture as an opponent of God. Viewing the larger landscape of all scripture, I believe that I can follow Jesus without being fettered by those archaic metaphors. I believe that it is more spiritually responsible to live my life realizing that Satan has no actual existence at all. There are, of course, times when it is tempting to blame my persistent failures upon some evil influence outside myself. However, I think it is safer to assume full responsibility for my actions.

The worst deceiver I have experienced is my own self, and the most horrendous evils of history are the deeds of other self-deceived persons. I am capable of perpetrating those same destructive deeds, and it is only by the grace of God that I have been spared from doing so. Indeed, in some misguided attempt to save the world from those who are, supposedly, in league with Satan, one might end up doing even greater damage. So I refuse to pass through the world trying to discern the good guys from the bad guys, finding demonic conspiracies. I have learned long since that the world's worst woes are the works of imperfectly evolved, dysfunctional persons. They need to be brought to justice, constrained, treated, if possible healed, or confined to institutions. Yes, there are bad people in our world; however, we will not make the world safe by demonizing them when we ought to be dealing with them firmly, justly, rationally, and with hopeful, healing operational strategies. We must set limits on the damage they can do to themselves and others and nurture them to wholeness if we can. That goes for individuals and nations.

So my day begins in the realization that our world is not out of control, with battle lines shifting back and forth in some imaginary conflict with the ethereal forces of darkness. Instead it is dominated solely by the loving providence of the One God of utterly sovereign grace. Before even getting out of bed, I find it more helpful to whisper the Hebrew words of the Shema, "Hear, O People of God: the LORD is our GOD, the LORD alone. We shall love the LORD our GOD with all our heart, with all our soul, and with all our might!" I live remembering the words carved over the entrance gate at the Abbey of Gethsemane, "God Alone." I am trying to learn what it is like to live with and for God alone, knowing that along my pathway there will be not only those special providences that appear suddenly at certain moments, but that our life in this world is one grand act of providence at every moment.

In Jesus Christ, God's providential sovereignty has become for me a deeply personal experience. The Spirit of Jesus is now spiritually at large in the entire world. This is made particularly clear in the Fourth Gospel with its unique teaching about the Paraclete, the Spirit of truth. The Gospel of John speaks to a generation in which most Christians were wondering when Jesus would return in cataclysmic judgment upon the whole world. Responding to this John's gospel fills us with the assurance that Jesus has not left us. On the eve of his execution, Jesus said to his friends, (John 14:19, 20) "In a little while the world will no longer see me, but you will see me; because I live, you also will live. On that day you will know that I am in my Father, and you in me, and I in you." As these assurances continue through John 14–16, we are assured that God's presence has "made its home" within us. Jesus is still with us as a guiding, teaching spiritual presence. For that matter (John 1:9), Jesus' Spirit is "the true light, which enlightens everyone." In some back room of every soul, a small candlelight of God's presence has not been extinguished. In a sense beyond our ability to discern or define it, God holds a firm beachhead in the variegated terrain of every life. Because I live in a God-haunted world, a world pervaded by God's gracious presence, I live my day seeking to be aware of how God may be working in every life. I consciously keep looking for how the Spirit will show up around the next corner, as Dr. Ellens says.

However, believing in God's radical, unconditional, and universally saving grace is not, as some people think, an "easy out," a soft-headed liberal escape from responsible discipleship. Quite the contrary, such radical grace calls us to a life that is both joyful and strenuous in its sense of mission.

To live believing that God will bring all of his children home at last is, as Quaker George Fox wrote, to "walk cheerfully over the world, answering that intimation of God in every one." I must learn to see the divine Spirit of Jesus coming toward me in every life. My life must become like a Benedictine monastery in which "All guests who present themselves are to be welcomed as Christ."[2] I find myself feeling like that aged doorkeeper of a western monastery who, whenever a knock came at the door, would say, "O Jesus, is that you again?" Left to my natural choices, not everyone who appears at the door of my life is someone I would choose as a friend. It is unrealistic to think that I can *like* everyone. However, because of God's gracious acceptance of all souls, I may not choose whom I will *love*. No matter how God-forsaken someone may appear, I try never to forget the words attributed to the Catholic theologian Paul Claudel, "There is no one of my brothers I can do without. In the heart of the meanest miser, the most squalid prostitute, the most miserable drunkard, there is an immortal soul with holy aspirations which, deprived of daylight, worships in the night." Our calling is to be the light of Christ's Spirit in those dark places.

2. *The Rule of Benedict* 53:1. Timothy Fry, ed., *The Rule of St. Benedict in English* (Collegeville, MN: Liturgical, 1982) 73.

And this means that I must deal hopefully with everyone. I must pray daily for the neighbor whose spiritual life is literally suffocated by racist hatred. Even though shunned by the entire neighborhood, I wave to him with a smile as he drives by every morning on his way to work. I speak to him with friendly hope. If some opportunity is given me to talk with him about my faith, I will not tell him that he is a lost sinner in need of salvation. I will try to find some words by which to express to him how much God loves him, believes in him, finds him interesting, and enjoys his unique gifts. I will tell him of the ways in which he can be a blessing to our neighborhood. I will speak to him as though he is already a believer. Christoph Blumhardt, whose faith and worldview influenced such major theologians as Karl Barth and Jürgen Moltmann, declared, "My father once wrote to me that I should make it a rule for myself at all times to view everyone as a believer, never to doubt it, and never to talk to a person in any other way . . . Every human being believes, because God believes in him."[3]

As strenuously as I may try to live with such hope and reverence for every life, I fully admit that it is exceedingly difficult to discern spiritual progress in the lives of some people. Judging by the surface of their lives, they seem hopelessly far from home spiritually. Some Christians might even view them as predestined to damnation. I cannot, however, accept the idea that anyone is impossible for God. I do not know how God will deal with the Hitlers and other monsters of history. But I believe that there is no hiding place from the presence of God even in eternity. The only place there is to go is into the presence of God whose purifying, purgatorial love will be for them "hell until it is heaven." God will purify even Hitler, and never torment any soul. His justice and mercy will bring every one of his children home at last.

George MacDonald said touchingly, "I believe that justice and mercy are simply one and the same thing; without justice to the full there can be no mercy, and without mercy to the full there can be no justice. God's mercy is so profound that he will hold his children in the consuming fire of his passion until they pay the uttermost farthing, until they drop the purse of selfishness with all the dross that is in it, and rush home to the Father and the Son, and the many brethren – rush inside the centre of the life-giving fire whose outer circles burn. I believe that no

---

3. Jürgen Moltmann, *The Coming of God*, trans. Margaret Koihl (Minneapolis: Fortress, 1996) 249.

hell will be lacking which would help the just mercy of God to redeem his children."[4] It is no light matter to live with such a faith, to realize that I cannot give up on any one of God's children, however hopeless they may seem to be. After all, without such divine justice and mercy, I am as hopeless as they are.

So I must live seeking such justice and mercy for everyone, especially for those whom Jesus called the "least of his brethren." He cared most for those for whom others cared least. I try to remember that those whom the world esteems least will be the very ones called to witness for or against me when I receive my final performance review. When I tutor Hispanic migrant children, I try to remember that I will see them again on some future day, and that my care and reverence for their lives will be the only true measure of the genuineness of my faith.

I have carried with me for many years a little book given to me by a simple country lady with very little education. She had cherished this book, almost as though it were her Bible. It is *The Greatest Thing in the World*, by Henry Drummond. I have quoted its final words in more sermons than I can remember.

> It is in the presence of *Humanity* that we shall be charged. The spectacle itself, the mere sight of it, will silently judge each one of us. Those will be there whom we have met and helped; or the unpitied multitude whom we neglected or despised. No other witness need be summoned. No other charge than lovelessness shall be proferred. Be not deceived. The words which all of us shall one Day hear will sound not of theology but of life, not of churches and saints but of the hungry and the poor, not of creeds and doctrines but of shelter and clothing, not of Bibles and prayer-books but of cups of cold water in the name of Christ."[5]

The final words of Robert Falcon Scott as that famous explorer lay dying with his comrades in the freezing wastes of the Antarctic, were simple, "Make him a strenuous man." He was leaving a message that he hoped would somehow reach his wife in England. It was his will and testament about the upbringing of their son, whom he would never see again. Were I to leave some last message to my own children I would urge

---

4. George MacDonald, *Unspoken Sermons* (1885; reprinted, Whitethorn, CA: Johannsen, 1997) 535.

5. Henry Drummond, *The Greatest Thing in the World* (New York: Crowell, 1894) 40, 41.

them to seek the kind of strenuous faith that is described in this book. The author has practiced just such a robust faith himself, as a courageous pastor who spoke his troubled truth even when a timid, tradition-bound denomination tried to silence him. He spoke it as a military chaplain on the field of battle. He speaks it still today as a therapist, preacher, and teacher, comforting and challenging clients, congregants, and students to seek this healthy realistic faith. I hope that this book will in some way move you, the reader, toward that same radically, grace-filled life of faith and discipleship.

About the Author and Respondents

J. HAROLD ELLENS, PhD, is Philosophy Professor Emeritus, Psychotherapist in private practice, Pastor Emeritus of the Presbyterian Church USA, Retired U.S. Army Colonel, and Research Scholar at the University of Michigan, Department of Near Eastern Studies. His current scholarly specialization is research on the Son of Man in the Fourth Gospel. He is widely known as an international lecturer on the interface between Psychology and Theology/Spirituality, the Executive Director Emeritus of the Christian Association for Psychological Studies International (CAPS), and the Founding Editor and Editor Emeritus of the *Journal for Psychology and Christianity*. He is the author or editor of 177 books and 167 professional journal articles. His most recent published volumes are: *Sex in the Bible, a New Consideration* (Westport, CT: Praeger, 2006); *Radical Grace: How Belief in a Benevolent God Benefits Our Health* (Westport, CT: Praeger, 2007); *Understanding Religious Experience: What the Bible Says About Spirituality* (Westport, CT: Praeger, 2007); *Text and Community: Essays in Honor of Bruce M. Metzger*, 2 vols. (Sheffield, UK: Sheffield Phoenix, 2007); *The Destructive Power of Religion: Violence in Judaism, Christianity, and Islam, Updated and Condensed* in 1 volume (Westport, CT: Praeger, 2007); *Miracles, God, Science, and Psychology in the Paranormal*, 3 vols. (Westport, CT: Praeger, 2008); and *The Healing Power of Spirituality: How Religion Helps Humans Thrive*, 3 vols. (Westport, CT: Praeger, 2008). He is the editor of the Praeger series on *Psychology, Religion, and Spirituality*.

JACK MILES, PhD, is Distinguished Professor of English and Religious Studies at the University of California at Irvine. He is the recipient of the Pulitzer Prize for his noted work, *God, A Biography* (New York: Knopf, 1995), and of the MacArthur Prize for distinguished scholarship. A former Jesuit, he studied at the Pontifical Gregorian College in Rome and at the Hebrew University in Jerusalem. His doctorate from Harvard is in Near Eastern Languages and Literature. He was a Guggenheim Fellow and Regents Lecturer at the University of California, Senior Assistant to the President of the Getty Museum, and columnist and member of the editorial board of the Los Angeles Times. His work has appeared in *Atlantic Monthly, Washington Post, Boston Globe, Harvard Theological Review, Commonweal, Tikkun, Cross Currents*, and other national publications, including *The Destructive Power of Religion: Violence in Judaism, Christianity, and Islam*, 4 vols. (J. Harold Ellens, ed., Westport, CT: Praeger, 2004). His work on the New Testament as literary narrative, *Christ: A Crisis in the Life of God* (New York: Knopf, 2001), is a companion volume to *God: A Biography*.

F. MORGAN ROBERTS, DD, HLD, LLD, served as a pastor in the Presbyterian Church (USA) for over fifty years, having held five pastorates and three interim pastorates. Upon retirement, he was named Pastor Emeritus of the Shadyside Presbyterian Church of Pittsburgh. Thereafter he served as Interim Director of Field Education and Adjunct Professor of Ministry and Homiletics at Louisville Presbyterian Theological Seminary. Dr. Roberts was educated at Colgate University, the National University of Mexico, and Princeton Theological Seminary. He has received five honorary doctoral degrees. He is a member of the Society of Biblical Literature and an Honorary Lifetime Member of the Board of Directors of Louisville Presbyterian Theological Seminary. He also served on the boards of Pittsburgh Theological Seminary, Pikeville College, and Westminster College. He is the author of a book of sermons titled *Are There Horses In Heaven?* (Lighthouse Point Press, 1996); "One Pastor's Journey Toward a Constructive and Healing Ministry." Vol. 1, *Personal Spirituality*, in *The Healing Power of Spirituality: How Faith Helps Humans Thrive*, edited by J. Harold Ellens, 6–18 (Westport, CT: Praeger, 2010); "Evil as a Pastor Sees It," vol. 1, *Definitions, History, and Development*, in *Explaining Evil*, edited by J. Harold Ellens, vols. 1–3 (Westport, CT: Praeger, 2010).

JAMES M. ROBINSON, ThD, is Director of the International Q Project at the Institute for Antiquity and Christianity and past Director of the Institute. He is also Emeritus Professor of New Testament at Claremont Graduate University and past President of the Society of Biblical Literature. Among his many publications are: *The Secrets of Judas: The Story of the Misunderstood Disciple and His Lost Gospel* (HarperSanFrancisco, 2006); *The Gospel of Jesus: In Search of the Original*

Good News (HarperSanFrancisco, 2005); *The Sayings Gospel Q: Collected Essays* (HarperSanFrancisco, 2006); *A New Quest of the Historical Jesus and Other Essays* (Fortress, 1983); *The Sayings Gospel Q in Greek and English* (Fortress, 2002); *The Sayings of Jesus* (Fortress, 2001); *The Critical Edition of Q* (Fortress, 2000); *The Nag Hammadi Library in English* (4th ed. Harper and Row, 1996); and the critical edition of *The Coptic Gnostic Library* (Brill, 1975–95).

Suggestions for Further Reading

J. Harold Ellens, editor. *The Destructive Power of Religion, Violence in Judaism, Christianity, and Islam*. Vols. 1–4. Westport: Praeger, 2004.

———, editor. *Psychology and the Bible: A New Way to Read the Scriptures* (with Wayne G. Rollins). Vols. 1–4. Westport: Praeger, 2004.

———. "Fundamentalism, Violence, and War." In *The Psychology of Resolving Global Conflicts: From War to Peace*, vols. 1–3, edited by Chris Stout and Mari Fitzduff, 143–55. Westport: Praeger, 2006.

———. "The Obscenity of War and the Imperative of the Lesser Evil." In *Just War and Jihad: Violence in Judaism, Christianity, and Islam*, edited by R. Joseph Hofmann. Amherst, NY: Prometheus, 2006.

———. *Sex in the Bible: A New Consideration*. Westport: Praeger, 2006.

———. "The Interface of Theology and Psychology." In *Psychology and Christianity Integration: Seminal Works that Shaped the Movement*, edited by Daryl H. Stevenson, Brian E. Eck, and Peter C. Hill. Batavia, IL: CAPS, 2007.

———. *Radical Grace: How Belief in a Benevolent God Benefits our Health*. Westport: Praeger, 2007.

———, editor. *The Destructive Power of Religion, Violence in Judaism, Christianity, and Islam, Revised and Condensed*. Westport: Praeger, 2007.

———. *Understanding Religious Experience: What the Bible Says about Spirituality*. Westport: Praeger, 2007.

———, editor. *Text and Community, Essays in Honor of Bruce M. Metzger*, vol. 1, *Interpreting the Text for the Community*; vol. 2, *Implementing the Text in the Community*. Sheffield: Sheffield Phoenix, 2007.

———, "Walter Wink and Hermeneutics." In *Enigmas and Powers: Engaging the work of Walter Wink for Classroom, Church, and World*, edited by Frederick W. Weidmann and David Seiple. Eugene, OR: Wipf & Stock, 2008.

———, editor. *Miracles: God, Science, and Psychology in the Paranormal*. Vols. 1–3. Westport: Praeger, 2008.

———. *The Spirituality of Sex*. Westport, CT: Praeger, 2009.

———, and John T. Greene, editors. *Probing the Frontiers of Biblical Studies*. Eugene, OR: Wipf & Stock, 2009.

———. "Death in the Psychology of Terrorism and Genocide." In *The Many Ways We Talk About Death in Contemporary Society*, edited by Margaret Souza, 191–206. Lewiston, NY: Edwin Mellen, 2009.

———. "Women as Religious Leaders." Vol. 1, ch. 13. In *Feminism and Women's Rights Worldwide*, edited by Michele Paludi, vols. 1–3. Westport, CT: Praeger, 2009.

———, with Michele Paludi, "Religious Discrimination." Vol. 3, ch. 2. In *Feminism and Women's Rights Worldwide*, edited by Michele Paludi, vols 1–3. Westport, CT: Praeger, 2010.

Suggestions for Further Reading

———. "Jesus' Apocalyptic Vision: The Psychodynamics of Delusion." In *The Jesus Project*, edited by Joseph Hoffman. Amherst, NY: Prometheus, 2010.

———. "Why Fundamentalism Incites Violence." In Ilona Skupińska-Løvset, *Acta Universitatis Lodziensis, Folia Archaeologica, 26, Papers on Values and Interrelations between Europe and the Near East in Antiquity*, Łódź: Wydawnictwo Uniwersytetu Łódzkiego, 2009.

———. *The Son of Man in the Gospel of John*. Sheffield: Sheffield, 2010.

———. "Jesus' Vision and Delusion." In *Christ Is Doing Fine, Thank You: Still Questing for Jesus*, edited by John T. Greene and Mishael Caspi. Lewiston, NY: Edwin Mellen, 2010.

———, editor. *The Healing Power of Spirituality*, vol. 1, *Personal Spirituality*; vol. 2, *Religion*; vol. 3, *Psychodynamics*. Westport, CT: Praeger, 2010.

———. "Dreams, Visions, and Delusions: Madness in Shakespeare." In *Dreams and Visions: An Interdisciplinary Enquiry*, in *Presenting the Past, Central Issues in Medieval and Early Modern Studies Across the Disciplines*, edited by Nancy Van Dusen. Leiden: Brill, 2010.

———. *Light from the Other Side*. Eugene, OR: Wipf & Stock, 2010.

———, translator. *Schleiermacher's Die Praktische Theologie: A Post-Modern Translation*. Lewiston, NY: Edwin Mellen, forthcoming.

Bibliography

Aden, LeRoy, and J. Harold Ellens, editors. *Turning Points in Pastoral Care: The Legacy of Anton Boisen and Seward Hiltner.* Grand Rapids: Baker, 1990.

Aristotle (240 BCE). *Nicomachean Ethics.* W. E. Ross, trans., revised by J. O Urmson, in Jonathan Barnes, ed., *The Complete Works of Aristotle, The Revised Oxford Translation*, Vol. Two, Bollingen Series LXXI.2. Princeton: Princeton University Press, 1984.

Augustine, Aurelius (390 CE). *On True Religion.* Edited by Whitney J. Oates, *Basic Writings of Saint Augustine*, vol. 1. New York: Random, 1948.

Beier, Matthias. *A Violent God-Image: An Introduction to the Work of Eugen Drewermann.* New York: Continuum, 2004.

Capps, Donald, and Janet L. Jacobs, editors. *The Struggle for Life: A Companion to William James's* The Varieties of Religious Experience, SSSR MS 9 (1995).

Carter, John D., and Bruce Narramore. *The Integration of Psychology and Theology: An Introduction.* Grand Rapids: Zondervan, 1979.

Cobb, John B., Jr. *Becoming a Thinking Christian.* Nashville: Abingdon, 1993.

———. *God and the World.* Philadelphia: Westminster, 1969.

———. *Process Theology as Political Theology.* Philadelphia: Westminster, 1982.

Cobb, John B., Jr., and Franklin I. Gamwell, editors. *Existence and Actuality: Conversations with Charles Hartshorne.* Chicago: University of Chicago Press, 1984.

Cobb, John B., Jr., and David Ray Griffin. *Process Theology: An Introductory Exposition.* Philadelphia: Westminster, 1976.

Drummond, Henry. *The Greatest Thing in the World.* New York: Crowell, 1894.

Edwards, David L. *The Honest To God Debate.* Philadelphia: Westminster, 1963.

Ellens, J. Harold. *The Destructive Power of Religion: Violence in Judaism, Christianity, and Islam, Condensed and Updated Edition.* Westport, CT: Praeger, 2007.

———. *God's Grace and Human Health.* Nashville: Abingdon, 1982.

———. *Radical Grace: How Belief in a Benevolent God Benefits Our Health.* Westport, CT: Praeger, 2007.

———. *Sex in the Bible: A New Consideration.* Westport, CT: Praeger, 2006.

———. *Understanding Religious Experiences: What the Bible Says about Spirituality.* Westport, CT: Praeger, 2008.

Fosdick, Harry Emerson. *A Great Time to Be Alive: Sermons on Christianity in Wartime.* New York: Harper, 1944.

———. *A Guide to Understanding the Bible: The Development of Ideas within the Old and New Testament.* New York: Harper, 1938.

Freud, Sigmund. *Selected Writings.* New York: Book of the Month Club, 1997.

Fry, Timothy, editor. *The Rule of St. Benedict in English.* Collegeville, MN: Liturgical, 1982.

Gerkin, Charles V. *The Living Human Document.* Nashville: Abingdon, 1984.

Griffin, David, and Thomas J. J. Altizer, editors. *John Cobb's Theology in Process*. Philadelphia: Westminster, 1977.

Gulley, Philip. *If the Churches were Christian: Recovering the Values of Jesus*. New York: HarperCollins, 2010.

Gungen, David L. *Constantine's Bible: Politics and the Making of the New Testament* Minneapolis: Fortress, 2006.

Jarrett, Bede. *Meditations for Living Fully*. New York: Sophia, 1915, reprinted 2005.

Jung, Carl Gustav. *Man and His Symbols*. Garden City, NY: Doubleday, 1964; reprinted 1971.

———. *Selected Writings*. New York: Book of the Month Club, 1997.

MacDonald, George. *Unspoken Sermons*. London: Longmans, Green, 1885. Reprinted: Whitethorn, CA: Johannsen, 1997.

Maier, Paul L., *Pontius Pilate, A Biographical Novel*. New York: Doubleday, 1968.

Malony, H. Newton, editor. *A Christian Existential Psychology: The Contributions of John G. Finch*. Lanham, MD: University Press of America, 1980.

———, editor. *Current Perspectives in the Psychology of Religion*. Grand Rapids: Eerdmans, 1977.

Moltmann, Jurgen. *The Coming of God: Christian Eschatology*. Minneapolis: Fortress, 1996.

Newman, John Henry Cardinal. *An Essay in Aid of a Grammar of Assent*. Garden City, NewYork: Doubleday, 1955.

Niebuhr, Reinhold. *Human Destiny*. In *The Nature and Destiny of Man*, 1 vol. edition. New York: Scribner's, 1943.

Robinson, James M. *The Gospel of Jesus*. San Francisco: HarperSanFrancisco, 2006.

———, editor. *The sayings of Jesus: The Sayings Gospel Q in English*. Facets. Minneapolis: Fortress, 2002.

Robinson, James M., Paul Hoffmann, and John S. Kloppenborg, editors. *The Critical Edition of Q*. Hermeneia Supplements. Minneapolis: Fortress, 2000.

Robinson, John A. T. *Explorations into God*. London: SCM, 1967.

———. *Honest to God*. Philadelphia: Westminster, 1963.

———. *The Human Face of God*. Philadelphia: Westminster Press, 1973.

———. *In the end God*. New York: Harper & Row, 1968.

Schrödinger, Eric. *What is Life, the Physical Aspects of the Living Cell*. Cambridge: Cambridge University Press, 1917. In 2000 an elegant boxed edition was published in London by the Folio Society.

Thielicke, Helmut. *The Waiting Father, Sermons on the Parables of Jesus*. Translated by John W. Doberstein. New York: Harper & Row, 1959.

Tracy, David, and John B. Cobb, Jr. *Talking About God: Doing Theology in the Context of Modern Pluralism*. New York: Seabury, 1983.

Wicks, Robert J., Richard D. Parsons, and Donald Capps. *Clinical Handbook of Pastoral Counseling*. 3 vols. New York: Paulist, 1985–1993.

Index

Aden, LeRoy, 102
Al-Qaeda, 92, 98, 101, 103
Allport, Gordon, 77
Altizer, Thomas J. J., 106
Aquinas, Thomas, 66
Aristotle, 63–64
Augustine, Aurelius, 65

Barth, Karl, 12, 68, 167
Beier, Matthias, 103
Benedict, St., 166
Blumhardt, Christoph, 167
Boisen, Anton, 102
Borg, Marcus, 11, 12, 14
Bultmann, Rudolf, 10
Bush, George W., 98

Caiaphas, 37
Calvin, John, 6
Capps, Donald, 102
Carter, John D., 103
Chalcedon, Council of, 5
Chochmah, 8, 21
Christian Association for
    Psychological Studies, 82
Christology, 13, 17
Cobb, John B., 105
Constantine, 140
Crossan, John Dominic, 11

Darwin, Charles, 4
Doberstein, John W., 111
Drewermann, Eugen, 103
Drummond, Henry, 168
Dungan, David L., 140

Easter Faith, 151–52
Ecumenical Councils, 5
Edwards, David L., 66
Elijah, 80
Ellens, J. Harold, 20, 102, 103, 106,
    142–44, 154, 157, 164, 166
1 *Enoch*, 29
Eusebius, 140

Finch, John, 103
Fosdick, Harry Emerson, 64
Fox, George, 166
Freud, Sigmund, 103
Funk, Robert, 10

Gamwell, Franklin I, 106
Gerkin, Charles V., 95
Gods, Sick, and Sick People, 95–100
Griffin, David R., 105, 106
Gulley, Philip, 154–55

Hartshorne, Charles, 106
Healing, Faith, 146–47
Healing the World, 10 steps, 99–100
Heidelberg Catechism, 20, 29
Heresy, 127–34
Hiltner, Seward, 102
Holy Spirit, xiii, 17, 21, 41, 43–50,
    58, 63, 66, 95, 134, 139, 143
Hoffmann, Paul, 11

Irenaeus, 7, 8
Islam, 90, 101

Jacobs, Janet L., 102
James, William, 77

Jarrett, Bede, 65
Jefferson, Thomas, 73
Jesus Seminar, 10
Jung, Carl, 103

Kloppenberg, John S., 11
Knohl, Israel, 31

Logos, 8, 21

MacDonald, George, 167
Mack, Burton L., 11
Maier, Paul L., 22
Malony, H. Newton, 103
Marcion, 141
Maritain, Jacques, 117–18
Marty, Martin, 117
Messiah Before Jesus, 32
Metzger, Bruce M., xi
Micah, 108–15
Miles, Jack, 137ff.
Mithraism, 14
Moltmann, Jürgen, 167
Moses, 79, 137

Narramore, Bruce, 103
Newman, John Henry Cardinal, 67
Nicea, Council of, 56, 140
Nicean Creed, 5, 6, 139, 141
Niebuhr, Reinhold, 69

Obsessive Compulsive Disorder, 91

Paige, John, 73, 75
Parsons, Richard D., 102
Piper, Otto, ix, 67
Pontius Pilate, 22, 37
Pope John XXIII, 23
Pope Leo X, 9, 11
Pope Pius IX, 9, 19, 20
Prodigal Son, 112–14, 127, 129

Q, Sayings Gospel of, 11, 143ff.
Qumran, 32
Qur'an, 67

Reign of God, 143ff.
Reimarus, 10
Ritschl, Albrecht, 10
Roberts, F. Morgan, 154
Robinson, James M., 10, 11, 38, 143
Robinson, J. A. T., 65
Rogers, Carl, 93

Schleiermacher, Friedrich, 6, 68
Schweitzer, Albert, 10
Schrödinger, Eric, 71
Scott, Robert Falcon, 168
Sheol (Hades, Underworld, Hell, Afterlife), 26, 28, 162
Smedes, Lewis, 120
Son of Man, 38, 39, 46
Sophia, 8, 21
South Africa, 81
Spinoza, Baruch, 6
Strauss, David Friedrich, 10
Sunflowers, The, 116

Time Magazine, 118–19
Theistic Evolution, 3
Thielicke, Helmut, 111
Tracy, David, 106
Trinity, Personal or Modal, 45

U.S. Army, 80
USS Thresher, 108

Van Houten, Esther, 83–84

Warfield, Benjamin Breckenridge, 50
Weiss, Johannes, 10
Wicks, Robert, 102
Wiesenthal, Simon, 116, 118
Wisdom, 21, 64

Zionism, 42, 43

www.ingramcontent.com/pod-product-compliance
Lightning Source LLC
Chambersburg PA
CBHW062044220426
43662CB00010B/1648